C000110401

GOD IS WITH US

What Near-Death and Other
Spiritually Transformative
Experiences Teach Us About God
and Afterlife

GOD IS
WITH US

What Near-Death and Other Spiritually Transformative Experiences Teach Us About God and Afterlife

BY

KEN R. VINCENT

www.whitecrowbooks.com

God Is With Us

Copyright © 2019 by Ken R. Vincent. All rights reserved.

Published in the United States of America and the United Kingdom by
White Crow Books; an imprint of White Crow Productions Ltd.

The right of Ken R. Vincent to be identified as the author of this work has been
asserted by him in accordance with the Copyright, Design and Patents act 1988.

No part of this book may be reproduced, copied or used in any form
or manner whatsoever without written permission, except in the
case of brief quotations in reviews and critical articles.

For information, contact White Crow Books
by e-mail at info@whitecrowbooks.com.

Cover Design by Astrid@Astridpaints.com
Interior design by Velin@Perseus-Design.com

Paperback ISBN 978-1-78677-101-8
eBook   ISBN 978-1-78677-102-5

Non-Fiction / Body, Mind & Spirit / Parapsychology / Near-
death experience / Religion / Universalism

www.whitecrowbooks.com

*This book is dedicated to my wife Pam
who is my best friend and first editor.*

CONTENTS

Acknowledgements

~

This book represents my lifetime as a spiritual seeker. Along the way, every relative, teacher, friend, mentor, and co-worker has contributed to my understanding. My father always showed kindness and tolerance uncharacteristic for his time; he was even open the spiritual teachings of his Masonic Lodge. My mother told me of her Universalist relatives who didn't believe in eternal hell. My Aunts Ene and Maxine were consistent examples of faith in practice. In my freshman year at Baylor, Prof. Kyle Yates introduced me to Zoroaster, prompting my fascination with comparative religion. Prof. John Cox and Prof. Susan Clevenger transformed me into a psychologist and social science researcher. Rev. Wes Seeliger was an Episcopal priest who— very early on the curve — got us Houstonians to help spread the word about new research into the historical Jesus. Dr. Pam Kircher, my friend and colleague, invited me to "sit in" during her near-death support group, and many of the participants allowed me to include them in my book *Visions of God*.

My heartfelt thanks goes to my friend Kevin Williams, webmaster for the long-standing and highly regarded website, www.near-death. com. A tireless advocate for Universalism, Kevin posted this book prominently on his website in 2014 and made it available for reading online or free downloads. This effort to "get the word out" has proved more successful than either of us had thought possible.

Finally, I want to thank Jon Beecher, a fellow seeker, who has agreed to produce this book in a hard-bound version for those people who, like me, still like to hold books in their hands.

Most importantly, I want to thank my wife Pam, who for the past 25 years has been turning my academic esoterica into reader-friendly prose.

Introduction

~

T his book is about God and the direct experience of God by human beings. My doctorate is in psychology, and I am committed to understanding the whole range of human experience. My expertise is in a field called transpersonal psychology which seeks to study scientifically these encounters with the transcendent. The terminology used for these mystical experiences is varied, and includes: transpersonal experience, spiritually transformative experience, religious experience, spiritual experience, peak experience, near-death experience (NDE), after-death communications (ADC), and cosmic consciousness. When I speak of religious experience, it is always from the perspective of psychology and not from that of theology.

Although people have been reporting their experiences of God and afterlife for all of recorded history, we now know more about these phenomena than ever, thanks to research by social scientists and biomedical specialists over the past 150 years using scientific methods of analysis, as they would for any other topic of inquiry. We can state unequivocally that persons who have these transpersonal experiences are normal and mentally healthy (and not psychotic). And while we do not have absolute proof that God communicates with humans and that there is life after death, we do now have evidence for both. So come with me on a journey of discovery! Who knows? You may, "become a true believer!"

All of the chapters were previously published in a journal or magazine. The following is a brief summary of each:

1. *The Search for God and Afterlife in the Age of Science* - NDEs and other transpersonal experiences point to the existence of

God, the nature of God, and personal consciousness following physical death.

2. *Developmental Revelation* – Parallels exist between the development of individual humans and the progress of whole cultures throughout history; evidence for this maturation process can be found in the stories of the world's religions.

3. *"Universals" In Religion* – Five "universals" are common to all religions.

4. *Separating the "Super" from the "Natural"* – What kind of miracles can we believe?

5. *Religious Experience of Jesus Compatible with Modern Research* – Modern scholarship on religious experience is used to separate mythology from reality regarding Jesus and his mystical experiences.

6. *Resurrection Appearances of Jesus as After-Death Communications (ADC)* – The "resurrection" appearances of Jesus described in the Bible are compatible with the phenomenology of modern ADCs.

7. *Resurrection Appearances of Jesus as ADC: Rejoinder to Gary Habermas* – A defense is offered to a Conservative Christian scholar/ critic who retains his view that Jesus's appearances are those of a "reanimated corpse."

8. *Religious Experience Research Reveals Universalist Principles* – Universalist principles recur in the writings of researchers of NDEs and other STEs.

9. *Mystical Religious Experiences and Christian Universalism* – Modern researchers in social sciences maintain that mystical experiences are quite common and that they reinforce what Jesus taught about God's love for everyone.

10. *The NDE and Christian Universalism* - Explores the NDE in context of Christian Universalism

11. *An Eighteenth-Century NDE: The Case of George de Benneville* – Presenting one of the most credible and documented cases of an NDE.

12. *Zoroaster: The First Universalist* – Zoroaster is known as the Prophet of the Magi whose theology entered the West through its influence on Judaism and Christianity.

13. *Omar Khayyam: Sufi Universalist* – Khayyám was a Sufi mystic from Persia whose Islamic Universalism was expressed through his poetic verses.

Come with me as we part the veil just a bit! If you are among the 50% of us who have had a spiritually transformative experience or near-death experience, I hope that you will find comfort in what I've written. If you are one of the 50% who have not yet had a personal spiritually transformative experience, I hope you will find knowledge of them illuminating. Truly, God is with us.

Dr. Ken R. Vincent

CHAPTER 1

The Search for God and Afterlife in the Age of Science

~

Transpersonal experiences involve perceptions that transcend the usual personal limits of space and/or time. Also known as "mystical experiences," "religious experiences," or "spiritual experiences," transpersonal experiences include: direct communication of humans with God or other divine beings; near-death experiences (NDEs); deathbed visions (DBVs); and after-death communications (ADCs). Individuals who restrict their study of transpersonal experiences to NDEs sometimes call other transpersonal experiences "near-death-like experiences" or, more awkwardly, "a near-death experience in which the person didn't die." Unlike parapsychologists, who try to explain paranormal phenomena, transpersonal psychologists focus on the anomalous experiences of non-psychotic individuals and the effects of these experiences on them.

By their nature, many transpersonal experiences point to the existence and nature of both God and an afterlife of continued personal consciousness beyond physical death. Scientific study of "transpersonal experiences" developed between the second half of the nineteenth century and the present (Basford, 1990, pp. viii-ix). Whereas William

James coined the term "transpersonal experience," Abraham Maslow greatly expanded the serious study of transpersonal experiences by deeming transpersonal psychology a "fourth force" in psychology after psychoanalysis, behaviorism, and humanism (Daniels, 2004, pp. 366-370).

In this paper, I will not address transpersonal experiences involving mediums, nor will I address faith healing, because I have not researched those areas. Rather, my focus will be the development of the study of near-death and near-death-like experiences over the past 150 years. I begin with a brief discussion of transpersonal experiences prior to the mid-nineteenth century.

Transpersonal Experiences Prior to 1850

All of human history is testimony to humanity's experience of the transpersonal. Prior to research into transpersonal experiences by biomedical researchers and social scientists, these accounts were often anecdotal and frequently "much-told tales." Twenty-five hundred years ago, Plato recorded the NDE of Er in his *Republic* (Plato, fourth century BC/1892). First-hand accounts from credible sources in the ancient world are rare. Zoroaster composed a poem that documented his direct experience of God (Vincent, 1999, pp. 91-127). St. Paul also told in his own writings of his life-transforming ADC of Jesus (I Cor 15:5-8). Additionally, St. Paul told of his out-of-body experience in which he was transported to the third level of Heaven (II Cor 12:2-5).

In the sixth century, St. Gregory the Great in Book 4 of his *Dialogues* (Gregory, sixth century AD/1959) provided a treasure-trove of transpersonal experiences including NDEs, ADCs, DBVs, and vivid dreams. These and other examples from ancient and medieval literature have some validity by the very fact that they sound so similar to modern transpersonal accounts; however, in almost all cases there is simply not enough in the ancient record to make a judgment on the veracity of the story. In her analysis of medieval and modern accounts of other-world journeys, Carol Zaleski (1987) noted, "we cannot simply peel away the literary wrapper and put our hand on an unembellished event, even when a vision actually did occur, it is likely to have been re-worked many times before being recorded" (pp. 86-88). She suggested, for example, that the Church would have been eager to insure that recorded accounts did not contradict "Truth" as defined by Church doctrine. Nevertheless, in the medieval world, first-hand accounts of transpersonal experiences became more commonly reported in the lives of the saints. A modern interdisciplinary collaboration between a historian and a psychiatrist into medieval transpersonal experiences revealed that visions appeared to have been related to mental illness in only 4 of the 134 cases the authors studied (Kroll & Bachrach, 1982).

First Period of Scientific Research into Transpersonal Experiences (1850s-1920s)

In the mid-nineteenth century, medicine was becoming a science. Physicians were rapidly learning about the human body, discovering that many of their long-revered treatments and medications were ineffective and/or toxic (Benson & Stark, 1997, pp. 109-114). Social sciences became a reality in large part due to the invention of modern statistics (Wood & Wood, 1996, p. 23). Concurrently, comparative religion emerged as a topic of study for the first time in the West since the classical period (Nigosian, 2000, pp. 412-413). This period witnessed the publication of Max Müller's *Sacred Books of the East* (1897) that enhanced Western knowledge of Eastern religion. Simultaneously, archeology was changing from a "treasure hunt" for adventurers into a methodical science (Oakes & Gahlin, 2003, pp. 26-41). In the mid-nineteenth century, physicians began to report DBVs and the rarer NDEs in their medical journals (Basford 1990, pp. 5-10,131-137; Walker & Serdahely, 1990, p. 108). Aided by social scientists, case studies and observations of transpersonal experiences began to be verified. In the 1880s, the Society for Psychical Research was formed in England, and shortly thereafter, the American Society for Psychical Research was founded (Cardeña, Lynn, & Krippner, 2000, p. 6). The membership of these bodies largely consisted of physicians, professors, and preachers. Its members were interested in interviewing subjects and assessing the credibility of case studies involving transpersonal experiences.

Ground-breaking studies produced by this new group of psychical researchers include Frederick Myers's *Human Personality and its Survival of Bodily Death* (1903) and Sir William Barrett's *Deathbed Visions* (1926). The following veridical account taken from Myers's classic work documents the infrequent phenomena of physical contact with a vision. It is the case of an appearance to Baron Basil Fredorovich von Driesen of his dead father-in-law with whom he had not been on good terms. The purpose of the father-in-law's ADC was for reconciliation. Basil reported shaking the apparition's hand which he described as "long and cold," after which the vision disappeared. The next day after the church service, the priest told Basil and his wife, "This night at 3:00, Nicholas Ivanovitch Ponomareff appeared to me and begged me to reconcile him to you." Thus, on the same night the son-in-law and the priest, at separate locations, saw a vision of the same dead man (Myers, 1903, pp. 40-42).

Another important study in the nineteenth century was Henry Sidgwick's *Report on the Census of Hallucinations* (Basford, 1990, p. 161). The British study included over 15,000 non-psychotic people and found roughly 10% of the participants reported apparitions, including ADCs and religious visions. This was also the case in a 1990s replication of the study using a representative sample of over 18,000 participants (Bentall, 2000, pp. 94-95). Although people with schizophrenia can and do report mystical experiences along with their psychosis (Siglag, 1986), more often than not people without mental illness report seeing religious figures whereas people with schizophrenia report being religious figures.

James Hyslop wrote many books on transpersonal experiences. His *Psychical Research and the Resurrection* (1908) is interesting. It includes not only veridical examples of ADCs and DBVs but also a treatise on the resurrection as an ADC in which Hyslop stated that "the existence of veridical apparitions would substantiate all that is useful in the story of the resurrection and make human experience in all ages akin" (p.383). This same approach, emphasizing that Jesus' resurrected body was (quoting St. Paul) a "spiritual" body (Hyslop, 1908, p. 377), was taken at mid-century by the Anglican Canon Michael Perry, who wrote *The Easter Enigma: An Essay on the Resurrection with Specific Reference to the Data of Psychical Research* (1959). This thesis was again raised at the end of the twentieth century by Phillip Wiebe who authored *Visions of Jesus* (1997). These and other modern authors made the case that post-resurrection appearances of Jesus are visionary experiences indistinguishable from ADC reports throughout history (Hick, 1993, pp. 41-44; Maxwell & Tschudin, 1990, pp. 66-67, 78, 105, 119, 150, 166, 168; Wiebe 1997, pp. 3-88).

The premier publication of the first period of research into transpersonal experiences was William James's *The Varieties of Religious Experience* published in 1902. In it, he boldly stated, "In one sense the personal religion [currently termed transpersonal or spiritual] will prove itself more fundamental than either theology or ecclesiasticism. Churches, when once established, live at second-hand upon tradition; but the founders of every church owed their power originally to the fact of their direct personal communication with the Divine. Not only the superhuman founders, the Christ, the Buddha, Mahomet, but all the originators of Christian sects, have been in this case; — so personal religion should still seem the primordial thing, even to those who continue to esteem it incomplete (James, 1902/1994, pp. 35-36;)." He went on to state that, "the difference in the natural 'fact' which most of us would assign as the first difference which the existence of a God ought to make would, I imagine, be personal immortality. Religion, in fact, for the great majority of our own race *means* immortality, and nothing else (James 1902/1994, p. 569)."

Further validation for James' assertion that the founders of every religion obtained the spiritual knowledge from direct transpersonal experiences of God can be found in Christopher Partridge's (2004, pp. 14-24) *New Religions*. Partridge listed over 200 religions that were founded or came to prominence in the last century; virtually all of their founders were transformed and inspired by a transpersonal experience such as a voice, a vision or other mystical experience of God, or an ADC from a religious figure.

Intermediate Period (1930s – 1950s) and Second Period (1960s to Present) of Scientific Research into Transpersonal Experiences

During the 1920's, research into transpersonal experiences began to wane. In my opinion, possible reasons for this include the death of the founders of research into transpersonal experience, the rise of atheism and Marxism culturally, and Freudianism and behaviorism in the social and biomedical sciences. In an article focusing exclusively on NDEs, Barbara Walker and William J. Serdahely (1990) noted the same "dry" period. Carl Jung (1961) became a lone "voice in the wilderness" regarding the importance of religious and spiritual experience in healthy human functioning.

As the father of humanistic psychology, Maslow revolutionized the study of psychology by emphasizing the healthy personality rather than psychopathology. Toward the end of his life, he went beyond this innovation by resurrecting James' term "transpersonal" and founding the field of transpersonal psychology (Maslow, 1964, pp. x – xi, 19 – 29; Partridge, 2004, pp. 366-370). During this same period, scientists had begun to use the electroencephalogram (EEG) to study meditation and other altered states of consciousness, demonstrating that meditative states were physiologically different from ordinary consciousness and not merely the "wishful thinking" of believers (Wulff, 1997, pp. 69-89, 95-116). Concurrently, the facilitation of religious experience using psychedelic drugs became the object of scientific study.

Timothy Leary was a respected professor of psychology at Harvard and one of the world's foremost researchers on personality at the time he began to experiment with LSD and other psychedelic drugs (Smith, 2000, p. 6). He did so in the best of company — with Huston Smith, a Methodist minister, theologian, and researcher on comparative religion, and Aldous Huxley, author of *Brave New World* and *The Doors of Perception* (Smith, 2000, p. 6). One of Timothy Leary's early research projects at Harvard was nicknamed his "Prisoners to Prophets" program (Leary, 1983, pp. 83-90). In this study, he supervised the administration of LSD to prisoners who were then followed after their release from jail. Initially, the LSD group had a lower recidivism rate than those in the control group who had not received psychedelic drugs. However, later these results were questioned, and it was suggested that their success could be better attributed to the interaction of the students with the prisoners, helping them readjust to society and helping them find jobs. In fact, a 34-year follow-up showed recidivism to be slightly higher for the LSD group (Horgan, 2003).

Leary sincerely thought he had discovered something beneficial to society: a shortcut that would enable everyone to become a mystic. Thus he was for some time the champion of psychedelic drugs. He and his sophisticated friends did not have negative experiences with LSD, and some had gleaned insights under its influence. Leary thought that the mystical experience was caused by the drug; sadly, the causality and dynamics of such experiences turned out not to be that simple.

I was an undergraduate student in psychology at the time this initial research was being carried out. One day, one of my professors came into class and announced that he was doing LSD research, and he wanted us all to take the drug as a part of his experiment. Now, this was in the days prior to strict guidelines for ethical research on human subjects, and it was not uncommon for professors to include among course requirements that students participate in their experiments. I was much relieved when my professor said that if we had jobs, we were not required to participate. He then went on to tell us that this stuff was SO good that he would give us some if we came to his office after class! He did caution that if we took it on our own, we had to promise to take it with a friend, as there were a few people who had "unusual side-effects." A few years later, after a number of people had experienced what came to be known as "bad trips," the Federal Government made psychedelics illegal. Clearly, the experience of God was not IN the drugs, as Leary had hoped.

About this time, a Harvard researcher named Walter Pahnke (Argyle, 2000, pp. 64-66; Smith, 2000, pp. 199-205) conducted a controlled experiment at Andover Theological Seminary in which he divided seminarians into two groups: one given psychedelics and the other given a placebo. He then put both groups into a two and a half hour Easter Service. The result was that a significant number of those given the psilocybin reported mystical experiences compared to the control group. What Pahnke had done was what shamans have done for centuries: use drugs to get their subjects "off-center." Psychedelic drugs induce perceptual distortions and force the subject out of one's normal mind-set, but it is the shaman – or, in case of Pahnke's experiment, the Christian ministers – who plays the critical role of guiding the experiencer. In the case of Native American shamans, the setting is a hogan where the participant is surrounded by fellow worshipers, fire, and chanting. In the Christian Easter service, the "Christian shamans" provided the context of music, liturgy, and prayer. The total spiritual setting is the "trigger" of the mystical experience; the drugs aid only to the extent that they allow the experiencer to step out of ordinary reality (Wulff, 1997, pp. 188-193). As Sufi mystic Abu Said (Vincent, 1994, p. 40) put it, "The way to God is but one step, the step outside yourself." In addition to the relationship between transpersonal experiences and psychedelic drugs, there is also some overlap between transpersonal experiences and psychosis. This was the focus of a recent book entitled, *Psychosis and Spirituality* (Clarke, 2001). Mysticism can be differentiated from psychosis through psychological assessment. Ralph Hood (2001, pp. 20-31) developed two scales to measure the in-depth nature of religious mystical experience: the Religious Experience Episode Measure (REEM) and the Mysticism Scale (M-Scale). These instruments separate mystics from non-mystics but do not clearly differentiate mystics from psychotics. To achieve the latter, a diagnostician needs also to use an instrument that differentiates people with and without psychosis. Use of more than one test for differential diagnosis is commonplace in psychology; for example, the diagnosis of learning disability requires administration of both reading and IQ assessments (Vincent, 1987, pp. 45-58).

Although it is possible to be both mystic and psychotic, modern research has uncovered many more people having mystical experiences than having psychoses (Argyle, 2000, pp. 71-72, Hood, 2001, pp. 410-411). These differences are further highlighted in a study using word analysis to differentiate the verbal descriptions of mystics, psychedelic drug users, psychotics, and people not included in any of those groups. The researchers found that the descriptions of the various experiences do not match (Oxman, Rosenberg, Schnurr, Tucker, & Gala, 1988). In general, studies on mysticism and mental health have consistently shown that the overwhelming majority of mystics are mentally "normal" or "healthy." In 1969, Sir Alister Hardy, a biologist, set up the Religious Experience Research Unit at Oxford University, now the Religious Experience Research Centre at the University of Wales, Lampeter (Rankin, 2008, p. 3). This venture marked the beginning of large-scale research into mystical experiences. In order to research mystical religious experience within the general population, Hardy made an appeal to the general public through newspapers and pamphlets with the question, "Have you ever been aware of or influenced by a presence or power, whether you call it 'God' or not, which is different from your everyday self?" He invited readers to send in their responses. Ten years later, Hardy (1979/1997) published a book based on the first 3,000 responses he had received to this question on mystical experiences.

Next, moving beyond self-selected sample methodology, researchers undertook large-scale survey research. In 1977, David Hay and Ann Morisy (Hardy, 1979/1997, pp. 124-130) asked the same question to a British national sample of 1,865 persons: 35% responded "yes." Between the times of the appeal in the British newspaper and the objective large-scale population survey, Andrew Greeley (1974) and his colleagues at the National Opinion Research Center at the University of Chicago began asking a very similar question: "Have you ever felt as though you were very close to a powerful spiritual force that seemed to lift you out of yourself?" A sample of 1,467 Americans showed 39% answered "yes." Over the years, repeated national samples have shown that the number of people responding affirmatively to this question has ranged from 35%-50% (Wood, 1989, p. 856). When respondents have been interviewed rather than surveyed, the number has increased to over 60% (Hay, 1987, pp. 136-137).

Possibly because more Americans are feeling more confident in their spirituality, or maybe because the question was phrased differently, when asked recently, "In general, how often would you say you had experienced God's presence or a spiritual force that felt very close to you?", 86% of Americans reported one or more transpersonal experiences. Who knows? Maybe we humans are coming "out of our (spiritual) closet" (Mitofsky International and Edison Media Research, 2002)! In the first 3,000 cases of mystical experiences that Hardy and his colleagues collected, one of the "triggers" of mystical experience "was the prospect of death." More recently, Mark Fox (2003, pp. 243-329) has analyzed these "crisis experiences" (CE) and compared them to other non-crisis mystical experiences (non-CE). Whereas most of these CEs were NDEs, it was hard to tell from the voluntary reports whether or not these individuals had died or, in some cases, only come close to death. In spite of this limitation, Fox conducted the study because these CE/NDEs had occurred prior to the popularization of the NDE. He found remarkable similarity between these two groups. In other words, one of the ways to have a mystical experience is to die! This link between the NDE and other mystical experiences is a commonly reported finding (Cressy, 1994, 1996; Fenwick & Fenwick, 1995, pp. 229-236; Kircher, 1995, pp. 81-91; Ring, 2005, pp. 51-52; Vincent, 1994, pp. 9-17).

Recently, Xinzhong Yao and Paul Badham of the Alister Hardy Research Centre have published a major research project entitled, *Religious Experience in Contemporary China* (2007). Yao and Badham surveyed 3,196 Chinese. Religion is suppressed in China, and it should be no surprise that few respondents indicated a religious affiliation, but 56.7% reported religious/spiritual experiences. Using Buddhism as an example, only 2.3% of the Chinese reported being Buddhist, but 27.4% said they had worshiped Buddha within the past year, and 18.2% reported a religious experience involving Buddha or bodhisattvas at some time during their lives (Holmes, 2006).

Another major cross-cultural study on transpersonal experiences is reported in Osis and Haraldsson's book *At the Hour of Death* (1977) which documents 1,708 cases of deathbed visions recorded by physicians and nurses in the United States and India. These researchers compared patients with deathbed visions to patients whose diagnosis would have resulted in psychotic hallucinations such as brain disease, uremia, and fever in excess of 103 degrees. They also took medication effects into account. The apparitions of the dying in both the U.S. and India involved dead relatives and religious figures; in no case, in either the U.S. pilot

13

study or the cross-cultural study, was the "take-away" person – the relative or religious figure whom the patient perceived had come to take the patient to the afterlife – an apparition of a living individual. In general, deathbed visions were similar in both countries, though there were some differences. One-tenth of the Americans and one-third of the Indians expressed negative emotions when religious figures appeared. Indians were more anxious about dying, probably because the Hindu religion teaches Judgment. However, once the dying experience began, it was almost always pleasant for both Indians and Americans. The only report of a person going to Hell was that of an Italian American woman. The most striking difference between deathbed experiences in the U.S. and India is one that could have been anticipated: the religious figures that came to take the person into the afterlife corresponded to the person's religion. Christians saw God, Jesus, angels, and Mary. Hindus saw such figures as Yamaraj, the Hindu god of death, as well as Krishna, Rama, and Durga, (Osis & Haraldsson, 1977, pp. 52-78, 218).

A byproduct of the Osis and Haraldsson study was that it included 120 people who were near-death experiencers (NDErs). Like the deathbed visioners, the NDErs in India and the U.S. had similar experiences. The one exception was that in the U.S., people reported being told to return or that they "had work to do." In India, they were apt to be told that their name was "not on the list." One Hindu reportedly was told by a Hindu messenger of death that they had brought the wrong person. Interestingly, this report included an account in which another man of the same name was in the same hospital, and when the initial patient regained consciousness, the other man with the same name died (Osis & Haraldsson, 1977, pp. 147-159).

Also in the 1970s, research was conducted on objectifying psychiatric diagnosis. The results of this research culminated in the *Diagnostic and Statistical Manual of Mental Disorders III* (DSM-III) in 1980. I was privileged to work on this project (American Psychiatric Association, 1980, p. 481). The DSM-III removed Freudian mythology from the diagnostic nomenclature and forbade a diagnostician to jump to a diagnosis based on a single symptom like hallucinations. More importantly, it acknowledged that religious experience was not in itself pathological; in other words, it was now OK for God to talk to you! In 1975, Raymond Moody published *Life After Life* and coined the term "near-death experience." Immediately after this publication, serious research into the NDE began. The International Association for Near-Death Studies (IANDS) was founded in November, 1977, by

Raymond Moody, Kenneth Ring, Bruce Greyson, Michael Sabom, John Audette, and a few others (International Association for Near-Death Studies, 2009). Research into the NDE quickly captured the attention of the public, overshadowing all other transpersonal experiences. This conclusion is evidenced by the sheer volume of NDE research (Holden, Greyson, & James, 2009, pp. 1 – 10). Highlights of serious research into NDEs include Ring's first objective analysis of NDE characteristics (1980). Shortly thereafter, Sabom (1982) carried out the first prospective study on the NDE. Ring and Sharon Cooper recently researched what the blind "see" when they have an NDE (Ring & Valarino, 1998, pp. 73-95). More recently, Jeffery Long and Paul Perry (2010) have published an analysis of 613 cases from Jeff and Jody Long's Near-Death Experience Research Foundation (NDERF) Website. One fruitful area of research has been into the aftereffects of NDEs and other transpersonal experiences. Briefly, the effects are overwhelmingly positive and life-changing, and they do not fade over time (Hay, 1987, pp. 153-167; Ring & Valarino 1998, pp. 123-144).

As questions have been raised regarding the NDE and its characteristics, scientific research has attempted to deal with them. For example, when the press consistently claimed that all NDEs were pleasurable experiences dominated by feelings such as peace, love, and joy, Greyson and Nancy Evans Bush (1992), in their article "Distressing Near-Death Experiences," countered with their analysis of experiences dominated by feelings such as isolation, torment, or guilt. When the astronomer Carl Sagan, acting as an arm-chair psychoanalyst, made the claim that NDEs were just people reliving their birth experiences, his "theory" was soon refuted in an article by Carl Becker that included data on not only newborn physiology but also the lack of similarity between features of the NDE and birth (Becker, 1982). In a study by Susan Blackmore (1983) entitled "Birth and OBE," she found no difference in reports of passing through a tunnel as a transition into another reality for persons born by Caesarean section or delivered vaginally. Finally, although the majority of NDEs are pleasurable, the process of birth is widely acknowledged to be traumatic. In all of recorded history, only one person is said to have laughed instead of crying at birth - Zoroaster (Vincent, 1999, p. 3). Sagan has not been the only skeptic of the NDE, but his case does illustrate that when questions are raised, scientific investigation follows. "Explanatory Models for Near-Death Experiences" by Greyson, Kelly and Kelly (2009, pp. 213-234) provides an excellent overview of research supporting and refuting claims about the origins of NDEs.

Michael Persinger offered more than theories on the NDE and other transpersonal phenomena (Kelly, Greyson, & Kelly, 2007, pp. 382-383). Using electromagnetic stimulation, he attempted to create NDE-type phenomena in the laboratory, and some of his subjects reported bits and pieces of phenomena similar to the NDE and other transpersonal experiences as well as extraneous phenomena such as dizziness and tingling (Greyson, 2000, p. 335). However, a recent Scandinavian study failed to replicate his findings (Keller, 2005). Based on Persinger's research, his student, Todd Murphy (2006), began marketing electronic devices to enhance meditative experiences. If transpersonal experiences could be safely induced in the laboratory using electrical stimulation, would this ability fulfill the age-old dream of giving everyone a mystical experience, change people for the better, and bring about a "new age?" On another note, Persinger expressed the belief that his research demonstrates that the NDE and other transpersonal experiences are located within the brain (Kelly, Greyson, & Kelly, 2007, pp. 382-384). However, brain stimulation can be interpreted as "cleansing the doors of perception" and leading to illumination (Kelly, 2007, pp. 603-607).

Since ancient times, people have attempted to induce transpersonal experiences. In the ancient world people used initiation into the "mysteries" (Meyer, 1987, pp. 3-13). Regarding the induction into the Mysteries of Isis, Apuleius gave an account that is in all probability autobiographical: "I approached the confines of death. I trod the threshold of Proserpine: and born through the elements I returned. At midnight I saw the sun shining in all its glory. I approached the gods below and the gods above, and I stood beside them, and I worshipped them." (Meyer, 1989, p. 199). He went on to state that he could not reveal more because it was a mystery! Historians have not established what percentage of people were able to have an induced transpersonal experience in the ancient world. The ancients' methods also are not known, but the idea that they had such knowledge continues to be intriguing (Ring, 1986).

In one attempt at induction, Moody invented the psychomanteum to facilitate ADCs in a non-intrusive way. Using a slightly tilted mirror, low light, a soft chair, and a dark room, Moody was able to create the condition for about half of his subjects to experience visits from their dead loved ones (Moody & Perry, 1993). This experiment has been replicated several times (Hastings et al., 2002; Roll, 2004). I am not alone among my colleagues in feeling that this modern-day necromancy is not without risks. If these visions are indeed real, as Moody noted

(1993, p. 112), the people who show up may not be the ones hoped for; if the apparitions are the products of the subject's unconscious mind, it is probably best to leave them undisturbed.

This brings us to another aspect of NDE research: religion and NDEs. Fox (2003, pp. 55-97) saw a deafening silence among theologians, who generally have not tackled the topic. This omission seems to be true for theologians in Christianity as well as other religions. However, Judith Cressy (1994), a minister and doctorally trained pastoral counselor, wrote linking the commonalities between NDEs and mysticism. Liberal Christian theologian Marcus Borg (1997, pp. 37-44, 171) has supported the validity of transpersonal experiences; he has also voiced tentative optimism about the validity of NDEs. John Hick, the world's foremost Universalist/Pluralist Christian theologian, is an enthusiastic endorser of transpersonal experiences and tentatively hopeful of the veracity of NDEs (Hick, 1999). Canadian theologian Tom Harpur has also addressed how multiple aspects of NDEs relate to Christianity in general, to specific Christian sects, and to world religion. He concluded his book *Life After Death* (1991) with a strong statement relating NDEs to Christian Universalist theology.

Outside of Christianity, endorsement for NDEs' relevance to religion is sparse. Some years ago, I was watching a television program in which the Dalai Lama was asked how NDEs affected his belief in reincarnation. He replied that NDEs reflect the "Bardo" state — in Buddhist theology, the intermediate state between death and rebirth. Recently, Zoroastrian priest Kersey Antia (2005) has written about Zoroastrianism, NDEs, and other transpersonal experiences. Writers on comparative religion have also written on the NDE. Zalesky's (1987) *Other World Journeys: Accounts of Near-Death Experience in Medieval and Modern Times,* Farnaz Masumian's (1995) *Life After Death: A Study of The Afterlife in World Religions,* and Gracia Fay Ellwood's (2001) *The Uttermost Deep* are good examples of books on NDEs and comparative religion. Recently, Gregory Shushan (2009) examined five ancient and culturally independent civilizations and concluded that the core elements of their afterlife beliefs are similar to those of NDEs. He stated, "Ultimately, this study points to a type of single experiential 'reality,' which may or may not indicate a single transcendental reality" (Shushan, 2009, p. 199). Warren Jefferson (2008) has written about the NDEs of North American Indians and documented that many of their afterlife accounts include reincarnation experiences. Finally, Marianne Rankin (2008) has written an excellent overview of transpersonal experiences, including

NDEs, entitled, *An Introduction to Religious and Spiritual Experience.* This work covers experiences in world religions, ancient and modern, East and West.

I have already discussed Osis and Haraldsson's (1977) wonderful comparison between Americans who were primarily Christian to East Indians who were primarily Hindu, but both authors were psychologists and not theologians. Some NDE researchers, including me, are not afraid to link findings from NDE research with their religious beliefs. These authors include Conservative Christians Maurice Rawlings (1978) and Michael Sabom (1998), Mormon Christian Craig Lundahl (1981), and Universalist Christians Ken Vincent (2003, 2005) and Kevin Williams (2002).

Conclusion

The search for God and afterlife in the Age of Science highlights an overlooked aspect of the so-called conflict between religion and science. For the past 150 years, social and biomedical scientists have researched the very nature of religion itself using all the tools available to modern science. NDEs and other transpersonal experiences can and are investigated in the same way all other psychological phenomena are investigated.

The validity of these experiences is based on several data sources, including:

(1) case studies of transpersonal experience (Bucke, 1901/1931, pp. 9-11, 287-289, 357-359; Guggenheim & Guggenheim, 1996; Maxwell & Schudin, 1990; Wiebe, 1997, pp. 40-88; 2000, pp. 119-141),

(2) sociological surveys that reveal who and what percentage of the population have NDEs and other transpersonal experiences (Argyle, 2000, p. 56; Wood 1989, p. 856),

(3) psychological assessment instruments that measure not only the mental health of the individual but also evaluate the depth of mystical experiences (Hood, 2001; Hood. Spilka, Hunsberger, & Gorsuch, 1996, pp. 183-272),

(4) biomedical and neuroscience testing, including the EEG, PET-scan, and functional MRI to, in some cases, document genuine altered states of consciousness and demonstrate that transpersonal experiences are not just wishful thinking (Hood et al., 1996, pp. 193-196; Newberg,

D'Aquili, & Rause, 2001; Wulff, 1997, pp. 169-188), and EEGs and EKGs that enable the documentation of the dying process in NDEs that occur in hospitals,

(5) sociological and psychological investigations that assess the after-effects these experiences have on people (Greyson, 2000, pp. 319-320; 345; Hick, 1999, pp. 163-170; Hood et al., 1996, pp. 410-411), and

(6) controlled experimental research such as Pahnke's experiment on the effects of psychedelics (Argyle, 2000, pp. 64-66; Smith, 2000, pp. 199-205).

In my opinion, although the NDE and other transpersonal experiences do not prove the existence of a personal God and afterlife, they definitely point to it. Research to date documents the fact that: (1) a large percentage of the population has experienced NDEs and other transpersonal experiences, (2) the overwhelming majority of those having NDEs and other transpersonal experiences are mentally healthy and not psychotic, and (3) NDEs and other transpersonal experiences change people's lives for the better. It also appears that NDEs and other transpersonal experiences represent phenomenological realities at the origin of virtually all the world's major religions.

CHAPTER 2

Developmental Revelation

"When I was a child, I spoke as a child, I thought as a child, I reasoned as a child, but when I became an adult I put away childish ways." (I Cor. 13:11) This familiar passage of St. Paul describes normal human development. My thesis is that there is a parallel between the development of the individual and the progress of whole cultures throughout history and that evidence for this maturation process can be found in the stories of the world's religions. Because the Bible documents a 2000-year period of human development, it is particularly rich with examples of developmental revelation.

There are many approaches to studying human development and religion, and these are reflected in the research of developmental psychologists like Jean Piaget, Erik Erikson, Jane Loevinger, and others. James Fowler, who is both a psychologist and theologian, devised a compelling list called, "Seven Stages of Faith Development."

The theory of human development with the most cross-cultural and comparative religious research to its credit (and my personal favorite) is that of Larry Kholberg. It is the one I have selected to explore with you in greater detail. To date, the consensus of his research shows that, when education and socioeconomic status are controlled for, human beings around the world from all faiths and cultures vary widely among themselves and that no faith or culture is clearly superior. According to Kholberg, there are three levels of moral development, each of which has two stages: Pre-conventional, Conventional, and Post-conventional. It is important to realize that not all people reach all stages of development, neither in the past nor today.

Pre-conventional

The "pre-conventional" level is the most remedial, and its first stage is called the "punishment and obedience orientation." This is the stage of pre-schoolers. The child at this stage lacks the mental structure to understand the rules but does understand rewards and punishment. Children at this age are not educable, but they are trainable. This is also the moral level of your dog or cat. Consider this example: At about age 3 or 4 years, your daughter has figured out that pushing the chair up to the kitchen counter will allow her to get to the cookie jar. Later, you come into the kitchen, see the chair and the empty cookie jar with its lid off, and you see the child with crumbs all over her face. When you ask, "Did you take the cookies?", your child gives the "right" answer—"No, I didn't take the cookies!" The parent is often devastated, assuming that his child is not only STEALING but LYING! The parent fails to realize that the child does not yet make the connection between cause and effect. Thankfully, very few adults remain stuck at this moral level.

In the Bible, the best-known example of this is the second Creation Story (Gen 2:4-3:24) in which you might substitute the "forbidden fruit" for the cookie jar. Adam takes no personal responsibility but blames Eve for giving him the fruit, and Eve blames the snake for her misbehavior! In the same story in Genesis, we are introduced to the oldest form of punishment—the banishment of Adam and Eve from Paradise. As demonstrated in the work of Jane Goodall, this links us with the behavior of baboons who banish members of their clan for "crimes" of dominance, sex, and murder. In the 5,000-year-old *Egyptian Book of the Dead*, this stage of morality is reflected in the behavior of the deceased who is expected to lie to the god Osiris in the Afterlife by reciting a magic formula known as the Negative Confession in which he denies all wrong-doing. We see this same magic formula in the Christian theology of "Jesus Saves." All one needs to know is John 3:16 and/or John 14:6. This is a gross distortion of the teachings of Jesus. Another Christian theology at this level is Predestination. In predestination, individuals cannot influence their own salvation and like the small child have no understanding of the reason for the rules. Before we leave the level of "magic" in human development, it is important to note that in times of distress, any of us may want a little magic! In Hinduism, it is said that if you die with the name of the god Vishnu or one of his incarnations like Rama or Krishna on your lips, all your sins will be taken away. Gandhi, who achieved the highest level of spiritual development, died with the name of Rama on his lips! The second stage of "pre-conventional morality" is that of reciprocity. This is the stage most of us reached in elementary school and is adopted to satisfy personal needs. At this stage, the rules exist to be manipulated. Children will give favors in order to get similar rewards in return. They discover that they can make "deals", i.e., "if you scratch my back, I'll scratch yours." A child will say, "I don't want to play that game. That is YOUR game, and we played that yesterday. Today is MY turn." Even in modern times, some adults get stuck at this stage.

Obviously, this level includes primitive religions in which an animal or human is sacrificed as a bribe to the gods with the understanding that the gods will do (or not do) something for the worshipers. Also, the idea in the *Hebrew* Bible that the righteous will always prosper, and that if something bad happens to you, it's because you have sinned belongs at this level. Some years ago, a student told me of working at an affluent church school that did not admit handicapped students because it was evidence that their parents had sinned. In the Book of Job, Job's friends express this view. The Prayer of Jabez is a "give me" prayer and at this level.

In the Bible, this level of morality is also represented in the law of "an eye for an eye and a tooth for a tooth" (Exodus 21:24). Getting stuck with this mentality can lead to barbarism and reminds us of the relentless retaliatory strikes we hear about on the evening news between the Israelis and Palestinians. Unless people are encouraged to higher levels of thinking, in the words of Martin Luther King, we are all at risk of becoming "blind and toothless." The only good thing about this rule is that you are only allowed to take one eye for one eye and one tooth for one tooth. Many of those to whom Moses preached were no doubt at either the first or second stage of "pre-conventional" morality—largely equivalent to that of today's small children. It also appears that the people addressed by Mohammed 2000 years later were at this level.

Conventional

The next level of moral reasoning is the "conventional" level which is reached by most people in adolescence; most adults never progress beyond one of its two stages. The first of these stages is the "good boy/ nice girl" phase in which "right" behaviors are the ones that please the person's reference groups, including family, friends, and peers. This is the first stage that goes beyond the manipulation of others for personal gratification and includes a genuine consideration for others. It is the first level at which the Golden Rule can be understood, if not practiced. In the Bible, the beautiful story of Ruth reflects this level of development when she declares, "Where you go I will go, and where you lodge I will lodge; your people shall be my people, and your God my God." (Ruth 1:16) Although this love passage is sometimes used for modern weddings, Ruth is not saying this to her husband—she is addressing her mother-in-law, Naomi. Ruth wants to remain with her mother-in-law because she loves her, not because she thinks Naomi's God is superior! This is the stage where the need for a personal god is strongest. In Hinduism this is the devotional path exemplified by the worshipers of Lord Krishna. "Krishna, Krishna, Hari, Hari": Krishna, Krishna, Redeemer, Redeemer. In Christianity, we see this manifested in those kind and loving people that model their lives on Jesus. One is reminded of the words of the beautiful old hymn, In the Garden: "and he walks with me and he talks with me and he tells me I am his own..." The second stage of the "conventional" level of morality is compatible with the view of "law and order." At this stage, morality is defined as "doing one's duty" and "obeying the rules." At this stage, rules are "right" because they have been formulated by one's superiors – a prophet, king, judge, president, or priest. This represents a step upward because, for the first time, the values of society as a whole are placed above the needs of the individual, his close family, or his friends. This is the mentality of "my country right or wrong." In the Bible, this is the mentality of the Ten Commandments (Ex 20:1-17) and represents the stern but fair God of Moses and Mohammed.

Returning to ancient Egyptian religion, the concept of the justice of weighing of the departed's good deeds is reinstated. As in Christianity, it co-exists with magic (e.g., *The Book of the Dead's* magic formula of Salvation and Christianity's "Jesus Saves"). The story appears of a grandson of Ramases II named Sa-Osiris, who is a seer, and his father. They were watching a funeral procession in which a rich man was being carried with his elaborate belongings to a princely tomb. Shortly after this, they observed the funeral of a poor man wrapped only in a cloth who was being taken for burial in the desert sand.

The Egyptian prince remarks to his son that he hopes for a good funeral in preparation for a glorious afterlife, but his seer son remarks that all things are not as they appear to be. He puts his father into a trance, and the two are transported to the land of the dead where the evil rich man is suffering a hellish fate and the righteous poor man is being comforted by Osiris, Isis, and the Egyptian gods, and is living afterlife in regal splendor.

This shows the development of morality and justice in the Egyptian religion, and some Christian scholars think this is the origin of the story of the rich man and Lazarus in the Gospel of Luke (Lk 16:19-31). The main point here is to underscore the great antiquity of the belief that salvation is by works. The idea that your good deeds must outweigh your bad deeds is found in all the worlds' major religions. In ancient Egypt it is Anubis, the jackal headed god, who holds the scales of justice, in Christianity it is the Archangel Michael, in Islam it is the Archangel Gabriel, in Zoroastrianism it is the angel Rashnu, and in both Hinduism and Buddhism it is the yamadoots of the god of death Yama. In the Eastern Religions, Yama presides over both your fate in the intermediate state between death and rebirth, and your reincarnation. It is worth noting that salvation by works is the predominant message in the New Testament with 389 of the 551 verses supporting it on the lips of Jesus himself. The Unitarian William Ellery Channing called it "salvation by character." According to Kholberg, MOST of humanity will remain at this "conventional" stage of moral development.

Post-conventional

Only one-third of humanity will reach the "post-conventional" level of morality. The first of its two stages is called, "the democratic social contract", and one-fourth of modern adults achieve this level. To these people, rules are obeyed because there is a consensus of the electorate. Also, the rules can be CHANGED whenever the majority of people agree to change them. The government of the United States is based on this level of morality, as were (to some extent) the governance of the early Christian church which, among other things, ordained women (Rom 16:1). While God's laws are unchangeable, the ways religions operate can and do change. Also, Process Theology fits here (i.e., the idea that God has endowed the Universe with free will and that we are co-creators with God). While Process Theology is a hot topic in today's divinity schools, the idea that we are co-creators with God in helping bring about the perfection of the world is as old as Zoroaster. In the New Testament, you find this idea in Acts 3:20-21 and II Peter 3:11-13. The final stage of "post-conventional" moral development is that of the "universal ethical principle", and only about 10% of humanity functions at this level. It recognizes a universal connection to nature, to each other, and to God. At this stage, the rights of each individual are as important as the rights of the majority, and the individual follows the dictates of his or her conscience while at the same time being aware of the rights of others. This person is aware that what is "right" and what is "legal" may not be the same and that the dictates of conscience must be followed. This stage is epitomized by the Golden Rule, often associated with Christianity but present in virtually all of modern mainstream religions. Zoroaster does not need to give his followers a commandment that prohibits murder — he does tell them that their good thoughts, words, and deeds are required to help God defeat evil in this world. Lao Tzu says, "Respond to anger with virtue", and the Buddha tells us to, "Overcome anger by love; overcome evil by good." Within Islam, the sect called Sufis strives to reach a sublime level of mystic union with God. A Sufi motto is, "It's not the letter, it's the spirit." In Judaism, this highest level is epitomized by the Book of Isaiah. Gandhi's tactics of civil disobedience were a good example of "post-conventional" thinking leading to action, making the world better.

In the Bible, the whole of Jesus' message of love and kindness speaks to this highest level. Think of the difficulty of his simple-sounding formula: "Do unto others as you would have them do to you ... Judge not ... Forgive and you will be forgiven. Blessed are the peacemakers ... Turn the other cheek ... Let him who is without sin cast the first stone ... love your enemies ... It is not what goes into your mouth but what comes out that is important." You may recall from stories in the New Testament that Jesus himself encounters people who clearly could not comprehend his message. More than once he simply refers them back to the Ten Commandments (Matt 19:16-20, Mk 10:17-20, Lk 18:18-20) or to the two Great Commandments, i.e., to love God and to love your neighbor (Matt 22:37-40, Mk 12:28-34, Lk 10:25-28). At the highest level: forgiveness is yours for the asking (Matt 6:12;7:7-11) and salvation is Universal (Matt 18:14, Lk 3:6; Jn 12:32; I Tim 4:10; Heb 10:15-17). Every mystic knows that we will all be reconciled with God, and Universal Restoration is a minority theme in all the world's religions. Zoroaster, Jesus, and Bahaullah mention universalism directly; the Rabbis of the midrash tell us that one cannot stay in Hell over one year! In the Hadith, Muhammad predicts that there will be a time when Hell is empty of humans. In Eastern religions, reincarnation offers the hope for universal redemption.

When we look at religions in modern times, it is clear that some have a broad appeal and others have a more narrow appeal. I think that the greatest risk for individual believers is to get "stuck" in a religious community that does not value personal growth. I have personally met people (including some ministers) whose intellect and spiritual experience have awakened them to a higher level of morality but whose congregations have discouraged or prohibited them from their pursuit.

In her analysis of the behavior of believers, the historian Laina Farhat-Holzman contends that some religious movements are accepting of persons at all levels of development and consciously make room for 1) those who base their belief on the "magic" of holy relics, 2) those whose religion is confined to ritual, and 3) those who struggle to understand the teachings of their prophets. Two excellent examples of religions that span the range of moral development from the lowest to highest levels are Roman Catholic Christianity and Hinduism.

In scholarly literature, the results of objective studies are mixed when analyzing the differences between denominations or religions. The most consistent finding has been that fundamentalists have a lower level of moral development than liberals. Interestingly, this appears to be true for those liberals professing no religion, as well as for those who practice Christianity or another religion. Some fundamentalist Christians have charged that these attempts at objective measurements have been biased; however, I believe that there is an alternate explanation.

Developmental psychologists have known for some time that people can truly understand only the moral stages just above and just below their own. Moses was above the masses of Jews of his time but NOT so far ahead that they could not understand him. Jesus was speaking to a more sophisticated group morally, one that had already been socialized by the "conventional" rules of Moses. In other words, Moses HAD to happen BEFORE Jesus could happen. If Jesus had confronted the people of the Exodus with, "Love thy neighbor ..." his message would not have been understood by them.

Often we religious liberals are hard on fundamentalists whom we accuse of being literal, concrete, and rule-bound. However, I must come to their defense with regard to this fact: these "conventional" people with specific messages are the ones most able to appeal to those at the level of "pre-conventional" morality and help raise them up. Although we reject their religious message and viewpoints, it is good to remember that humanity must crawl before it can walk. Years ago, an optimistic friend of mine questioned a fundamentalist who explained that, "We are fundamentalists because we NEED the tight controls of a 'Thou Shalt Not' morality; otherwise, we would go wild!" Another important truism for religious liberals to remember is that ALL children must pass through ALL stages of morality. No matter how intelligent your child may be, her moral maturity cannot be inherited at birth! All children need to experience structure and kindness so that they can develop to the stage where the Golden Rule can be understood and, ultimately, to the level where it can be lived. Research into how to accomplish this is mixed, but activities which require reasoning and exploration of moral issues appear to foster a progression toward the "post-conventional" level. Adults who have had an opportunity in college to explore moral issues must continue to find forums for discussion, reasoning, and moral growth. I think that this is an excellent challenge for Sunday Schools and Adult Education programs in our churches!

In closing, I'd like to express my own opinion about developmental revelation expressed in the Biblical stories. Although the stories of the Old Testament are part of our literary culture, Christianity has wallowed too long in their primitive "pre-conventional" morality. And although there is nothing more beautiful than the declaration of St. Paul that "love is patient and kind", many churches have allowed themselves to stagnate in his largely "conventional" message. In the recent past, a movement has been gradually growing which takes seriously the "post-conventional" morality of the teachings of Jesus in the Gospels. In my view, this should be the predominant message heard in our churches, inspiring people to "climb up" to the next rung on the moral ladder. But it's easier to worship Jesus than to follow his teachings. The "post-conventional" morality of Jesus demands that we live in the Kingdom of God RIGHT NOW – that it is possible to be ONE with the Father. In the Gospel of Luke (17:21), Jesus proclaims that, "The Kingdom of God is within you." We need to call it forth for the sake of ourselves, for the sake of all humanity, and for the sake of our whole planet.

CHAPTER 3

"Universals" in Religion

It is my nature to see the forest rather than the trees. Indoctrinated in the discipline of social science, my automatic response to any claim of "truth" is usually, "Where's your data?" So when it comes to world religion, it should not be surprising that I've been on a life-long quest to find the "universal truths" common to them all.

Before I begin, I'd like to share some of the vital events in my own religious life that may help to explain the metamorphosis into mystic and Universalist. During my childhood, I loved wandering in the pasture of my family's West Texas ranch where I became a "junior mystic third class." God's presence was always with me there (although I knew it was my own responsibility to watch out for rattlesnakes)! About the same time, I first learned of religions different from my own Methodist doctrine when three of my best friends told me they were Jewish. Some grown-ups contended that God would condemn my non-Christian friends to eternal hell, but I knew that idea was clearly incompatible with the God in the pasture! My own parents countered that they thought my Jewish friends would go to Heaven, but my Great Aunt Alice—who was a Universalist—went one step further. She was positive that ALL people went to Heaven! Even though she couldn't explain the theology behind Universalism, she had planted the concept of Universalism in my growing brain and heart.

Fast forward to my freshman year at Baylor University where I took the required religion classes. Reading the Bible, I discovered that the dogma emphasized by the denomination was either absent or contradictory. Jesus liked to eat well and drink alcohol, and the Trinity could not be found. Also, there was no mention of abortion at all! Instead of morphing into a nice conservative Christian, I became a Unitarian at age 18—what we in Developmental Psychology call a "lateral" change. My developmental level had not increased; I had merely changed perspective. During this "Taliban" phase as a new Unitarian, I would fanaticize about climbing to the ceiling of the Sistine Chapel to destroy the image of God as an old man and replace it with God as pure LIGHT! Two very positive things did happen at Baylor. First, I was introduced to Zoroaster—wonderful, wonderful Zoroaster! It was the first time I'd realized that God talked to somebody who wasn't a Jew! Second, I discovered Omar Khayyam, the Sufi mystic with an "attitude." My search for the "generic" God had begun! Many years have passed, and I can say with some assurance that I've graduated to "senior mystic second class," but my quest is far from over.

Whether the high God (or if you prefer Ultimate Reality) connects with creation in a personal way or not, there are two things that are true about God: God is REALLY BIG and God LIKES CHANGE! The further our science "sees" into the universe and our physics postulates other realities, the bigger God becomes. Change is a constant in the universe, and the only thing that is permanent is God. For clarity, it is important to understand that all my references to "God" should be understood as a "generic" God. Some people have difficulty using the word "God," usually because it conjures up images of a scary God who is angry and judgmental. Jesus called God, "Father/Abba," an affectionate, personal term. In world religions, God has many names: Ahura Mazda, Allah, Brahman, Tao, Yahweh, etc. These names are "God" in ethnic garb. In the twentieth century, it became fashionable to come up with alternative names for God, such as "Ultimate Reality," "Ground of Being," "Holy Other," or my personal favorite which appeared in the *UU World* a few years ago, "The Evolutor!" So feel free to translate your favorite word for "God" when I say, "God." Some folks like to claim that their religion offers the one, exclusive path to God. But confining God to one religion would automatically make God small, petty, and in a very real way, evil. The God of the mystics and the God of religious revelation is constant. Fundamentally, the trappings of culture and the limitations of language are what make one religion different from another. So any "truth" about God in world religion must be universal or nearly universal. Right now, you probably realize that this is going to be a VERY short list. So, as promised, here are the five things that I find to be "universals" in world religion:

1. Spiritually transformative experiences,
2. Prayer/Meditation,
3. The Golden Rule,
4. Faith healing, and
5. Miracle stories.

Spiritually Transformative Experiences

Virtually all religions are based on spiritually transformative experiences a.k.a. mystical/religious/spiritual experiences. These experiences are the basis for their founder's authority, and one need only look at Christopher Partridge's book *New Religions* to see that this is still true. Religion itself continues in large part because a substantial number of believers have their own mystical experiences, and this has been demonstrated by over 100 years of scientific research. William James' classic work, *The Varieties of Religious Experience*, was published in 1901 but is still in print today. Using the basic tools of observation and case studies, he began to research religious visions and mystical experience. James was able to formulate some working hypotheses on the nature of religious experiences, and many of these have been validated by subsequent research projects.

The big news today in the study of spiritually transformative experiences is sheer numbers! Social scientists now have documented thousands of people who have come forward to tell of their direct experience of God. Large-scale surveys on mystical experience began in 1969 when Alister Hardy founded the Religious Experience Research Unit at Oxford University. In order to research mystical religious experience within the general population, Sir Hardy made an appeal to the general public via newspapers and pamphlets which asked the question, *"Have you ever been aware of or influenced by a presence or power, whether you call it 'God' or not, which is different from your everyday self?"* Readers were invited to send him their responses. Ten years later, Hardy published *The Spiritual Nature of Man* based on the first 3,000 responses he had received to this question (of which 95% were positive). Over the years, organizations like the Alister Hardy Religious Experience Research Center, the Gallup Poll, and the

National Opinion Research Center at the University of Chicago have found the numbers of people responding positively to survey questions on religious experience in developed countries range from 35-50%. When people are interviewed rather than surveyed, the response rate goes up to around 65%. In one study, one-fourth of the respondents reported that they had never told anyone else of this experience for fear of being thought "mentally ill" or "stupid." Xinzhong Yao and Paul Badham have completed a major research project entitled, *Religious Experience in Contemporary China*. They surveyed 3,196 Chinese using a semi-structured questionnaire. Since religion is suppressed in China, it should be no surprise that few gave a religious affiliation; however, 56.7% reported religious/spiritual experiences. Using Buddhism as an example, only 2.3% of the Chinese reported being Buddhist, but 27.4% said they had worshiped Buddha within the past year and 18.2% reported a religious experience involving Buddha or bodhisattvas at some time during their lives.

Spiritually transformative experiences that point to an afterlife (e.g. near-death experiences, deathbed visions, and after-death communications) also show a remarkable similarity across time and culture. Regarding afterlife, the unresolved difference is reincarnation, even though it retains a minority opinion in virtually all religions. In one of the most important cross-cultural studies ever done on spiritually transformative experiences, Osis and Haraldsson's *At the Hour of Death* documents 1,708 cases of deathbed visions recorded by physicians and nurses in the United States and India. The study also included 120 near-death experiences. The apparitions of the dying in both the U. S. and India primarily involved dead relatives and religious figures, and in NO case in both the U. S. pilot study and the cross-cultural study was the "take-away" person (the relative or religious figure who came to take the patient to the afterlife) an apparition of a living individual. It should be noted that virtually all reincarnation religions have an intermediate state of Heaven and Hell before rebirth. In general, deathbed visions were similar in both countries, but there were some differences. The most striking difference was that the religious figures that came to take the person into the afterlife corresponded to the person's religion. Christians saw God, Jesus, angels, and Mary; Hindus saw Yamaraj (the Hindu god of death), as well as Krishna, Rama, Durga, etc.

Regarding the research to date on spiritually transformative experiences, it is valid to say that:

1. They happen to a large percent of the population,
2. The overwhelming majority of those people are normal, healthy, and no more apt to be mentally ill than the general population, and
3. They change people's lives for the better.

Prayer/Meditation

Virtually all religions practice prayer and/or meditation. Interestingly, there are religions that believe that the high God does not communicate with humans. This is true of most all Buddhists, many Hindus, and Unitarian Deists. In these religions, religious experience (e.g. Buddha's' enlightenment) is possible because it is put into the workings of the universe, and prayer is to lesser divine beings. It is important to realize that the angels, saints, and jinn of the West are the small "g" gods of the East because they perform the same functions. Some of these lesser gods/angels were created by the high God, but most of the entities prayed to around the world are dead humans. Humans have worshiped the dead since the beginning of recorded history and quite probably before. Two dead humans, Osiris and Isis, were worshiped by the ancient Egyptians for over 3,500 years and are still worshiped by some New Agers. One should remember that Roman Catholics who make up 2/3 of all Christians pray not only to God and Jesus, but also to the saints and angels. Jesus and St. Mary are dead humans; so are Lord Krishna, Rama and Seta, the Amida Buddha. Rama and Krishna have a similar relationship to Vishnu of the Hindu trinity as Jesus does with the Cosmic Christ of the Christian Trinity.

When people pray to lesser divinities, it would appear that the ancient Hindu idea that all sincere worship to God in all God's forms is acceptable and heard. The Bhagavad-Gita (7.21) says, "Whatever form any devotee with faith wishes to worship Me, I make that faith of his steady." Also as John Hick points out in his book *Disputed Questions*, "A second possibility (the first being atheism) is that of religious exclusivism; our own God—whether we be Jew or Christian, Hindu or Moslem—exists, whilst the others are figments of the human imagination. This possibility, however, is rendered implausible, in my view, by the fact that the effects in human life of devotion to these different Gods are so similar—both the good effect of the overcoming of self-centeredness and the growth of love and compassion."

The Golden Rule

Virtually all religions have a positive or negative statement of the Golden Rule: "Treat others as you want to be treated." I am indebted to John Hick and John Morgan for continually pointing this out.

Faith Healing

Faith healing is universal if you include healing prayer. In their 800-page book, *Irreducible Mind*, Edward Kelly, et al. devote 124 pages to psychophysiological influences, many of which are directly or indirectly related to faith healing. The short answer is: If you pray for yourself, it does help. The data are mixed about other folks praying for you. Also, there are some rare individuals who appear to be gifted with genuine healing abilities. For whatever reason, Rasputin could stop the bleeding of the little prince, but there is no record that he could will a severed arm to grow back. If meditation is added to prayer, even more positive research has been published, as in Mario Beauregard and Denyse O' Leary's book, *The Spiritual Brain*. In *Wondrous Events*, James Mc Clenon notes that indigenous priests and shamans often supplement what appears to be genuine psychosomatic healing with fraud and trickery.

Miracles

As Kenneth Woodward's *Book of Miracles* demonstrates, all major religions have miracle stories, not only in their ancient holy books but also in their ongoing literature. There are stories of a rabbi bringing a child back from the dead, a Christian monk using a holy relic to do the same, and a Sufi named Habib walking on water. A Hindu saint named Shankara assumed the body of a dead king, brought it back to life and ruled in his stead for a while. The special powers of Buddhist yogis include: flying through the air, walking through walls, and the ability to disappear. Prior to the Age of Enlightenment in the West, truly supernatural miracles like Moses parting the water, Jesus walking on water, and Buddha levitating and gliding over the water could be found in all religions. Interestingly, the few actual writings by the ancient mystics themselves don't include truly supernatural miracles. St. Paul is a good example of this; although he based his authority on his own spiritually transformative experiences (I Cor 15:8, II Cor 12:2-4, Gal 1:11-12, 15-17), his letters describe no miracles. Contrast what St. Paul wrote about himself with what was written about him in the Acts of the Apostles where he performs numerous miracles, including raising the dead (Acts 20:9-12).

Religious Practices That Are NOT Universal

Psychic powers such as mediums and divination are part of some religions but are not universal. The use of placebos when practiced by physicians is not "religious" faith healing. Charity and social justice programs exist independent of religious organizations, as do social clubs.

As mentioned earlier, there is a lot about religion that is NOT about God but IS about culture, and for many people, their religion and culture are inseparable. It is all right for religion to have cultural elements, provided they are not evil or destructive, but it is important to know the difference. When you read genuine first-hand accounts of spiritually transformative experiences—whether they are ancient, medieval, or modern—one thing that becomes abundantly clear is that God rarely provides details. Examples of human embellishment to religious practice include fasting, circumcision, self-flagellation, and abstinence from certain foods, alcohol, or sex. It is obvious the religious rules in books like Leviticus were written by priests in need of Prozac! Additionally, they often enable the person following the rules to feel "holier than thou" and to judge those disobeying the rules to be less favored by God. In contrast to cultural rituals that serve to say you are in the "club," the Golden Rule serves everyone.

Conclusion

To summarize, when thinking broadly about the "universals" common to all religions, the most important is the spiritually transformative experience—the very basis of all religion. Prophets, gurus, and saviors base their authority on them, and the spiritually transformative experiences of ordinary people help sustain religion. In fact, without spiritually transformative experiences religion would probably cease to exist. Second, prayer and/or meditation enrich the lives of those who practice it. Third, the Golden Rule is the essence of mature religion in practice. Fourth, faith healing appears to help some people, although how it works is far from settled. And fifth, miracles will always impress the naïve and uneducated, but we all can enjoy them from the standpoint of mythic reality.

CHAPTER 4

Separating the "Super" from the "Natural"

~

S upernatural means, literally, "over or above nature" but is commonly understood as an event that transcends the Laws of Nature. For millennia, all of nature's fury, blessings, and awesome mysteries were attributed to the gods or God. In most religious writings, however, we also encounter those "miracles" in which a Divine hand intervenes to contradict nature's laws.

In the mid-nineteenth century, researchers began to apply the scientific method to the phenomenon of religious experience. Biomedical science dissected the underpinnings of "faith healing," "placebo effect," "voodoo effects," and other aspects of cures for psychosomatic illnesses. Psychical researchers explored religious phenomena such as exorcisms. At the turn of the century, William James in his classic work *Varieties of Religious Experience* stated that, "the *founders* of every church owe their power originally to the fact of their direct personal communication with the Divine." In the 1970's, Sir Alister Hardy's *The Spiritual Nature of Man* demonstrated that—far from being the realm of a few saints, prophets, and sages—religious experiences occur in a large percentage of the general population. Over the years, an enormous amount of research has been undertaken into life after death, deathbed visions, after-death communications, near-death experiences, and reincarnation. Today, there is ample evidence of religious experience, a tremendous amount of anecdotal evidence pointing to an afterlife, data on psychosomatic research relating to faith healing, and some research relating to exorcism. Through the efforts of interdisciplinary science, we now know that religious experiences are not only "natural" but rather common. Conversely, truly nature-defying "miracles" are simply not present in the modern world.

In this paper, I will show how the "super" and the "natural" can be separated when the same standards of analysis are applied to both ancient and modern accounts. To illustrate, I have selected three famous religious persons from history: Zoroaster, St. Paul, and Muhammad. Zoroaster is the ancient Persian prophet who is credited with the divergence of religious approaches in the East and West, as well as providing the roots for subsequent Western religions—including the concepts of angels, demons, Heaven, Hell, Satan, and the resurrection of the body. Highly ethical for its time, Zoroaster's new religion advocated that man's free will to choose "Good Thoughts, Good Words, and Good Deeds" helps defeat evil. Like Moses and Buddha, the dates of his life are uncertain; a date of seventh century BCE is often given, although the archaic language used in his hymns to God suggests a date as early as 1600-1200 BCE. The first of his revelations occurred at age 15 years, but his major revelations occurred at age 30 when he, like Jesus, went into the wilderness to seek God. Virtually all scholars, ancient and modern, agree that Zoroaster himself is the author of his hymns *(Gathas)*. In them, he tells us that it was revealed to him "that silent meditation is best for attaining spiritual enlightenment" (Yasna 43.15). Zoroaster also says that God is supreme: "When I held you in my very eyes, then I realized you in my mind, O Mazda (God), as the first and also the last for all eternity, as the Father of Good Thoughts, as the Creator of Righteousness and Lord over the actions of life" (Yasna 31:8). At the end of our lives, our own good deeds will determine whether we go to Heaven or Hell; at the end of time, after those who are evil are purified in Hell, ALL will be saved (Yasna 30:11). Zoroaster's religious experiences of God were similar to those of mystics of all ages. Only after his death are "miraculous" tales attached to him—beginning with his birth. Later accounts in the *Avesta* (the Holy Book of the Magi) and the *Zand* (a Talmud-like continuance of holy writings) tell of exorcisms and miracles being performed by Zoroaster, beginning in his childhood (similar to stories of Jesus' childhood in the Apocryphal gospels).

St. Paul's religious experiences include his after-death communication with Jesus (I Cor 15:8), his out-of-body experience in which he is taken to the third level of Heaven (II Cor 12:2-4), and his speaking in tongues (I Cor 14:18). He states frankly that the Gospel (Good News) that he preaches did not come from humans but was communicated to him by Jesus from beyond the grave (Gal 1:11-12, 15-17). Paul both acknowledges and encourages the religious experiences of others (I Cor 12:8-11; 14:26-33). While he says that others have the ability to heal (I Cor 12:9), his letters do not tell of his healing; in fact, Paul writes that he was not even able to heal himself (II Cor 12:7-9).

Contrast Paul's own letters with the stories about him in the Acts of the Apostles (thought to have been written by the author of the Gospel of Luke). In *Acts*, Paul performs a negative miracle by temporarily blinding a sorcerer (Acts 13:8-11)—an excellent example of the "nocebo" effect (negative counterpart to "placebo"). Paul heals a man who was crippled from birth (Acts 14:8-10) and even raises the dead (Acts 20:9-12). Clearly, this author's depiction of Paul is very different from what Paul said about himself.

The final example comes at the end of the Classical World with Muhammad. His teachings were memorized by some of his followers, and others who were literate transcribed them. (According to Karen Armstrong, the Quran was compiled and edited some 20 years after Muhammad's death.) Muhammad works no miracles in the Quran, although he does mention miracles of past prophets. Interestingly, he includes the story of the child Jesus who made clay birds miraculously come alive (Quran 5:110). Although not in the New Testament, this story can be found in several apocryphal infancy gospels, including the Infancy Gospel of Thomas (2:4-8). In the Quran, Muhammad tells of his religious experiences of God through the Angel Gabriel (Quran 96) and his "dark night of the soul" when he had no revelations for two years (Quran 93). Muhammad describes his out-of-body experience, known as the "Night Journey," in which he is transported to Heaven (Quran 17:1). Interestingly, Aisha, one of Muhammad's wives, testified that his physical body remained next to her during this out-of-body experience.

Although Muhammad's religious experiences can be compared to those of persons today, the Hadith (later oral history) proclaims Muhammad a miracle-worker! The Moslem theologian Al-Ghazzali lists 45 miracles, including Mohammad feeding an army with a handful of dates, his blinding an entire enemy army by throwing a handful of dust, and his restoring the eye of one of his companions. Even better—Muhammad was given a miraculous birth! Our three ancient examples—Zoroaster, St. Paul, and Muhammad—suggest that ancient religious experience existed without supernatural occurrences. Buddha said that supernatural miracles were "for the uninitiated." Nevertheless, according to Max Muller, editor of the *Sacred Books of the East*, miracles are part and parcel of religion. To the unsophisticated of the world, belief in supernatural miracles and the magical power of religious icons remains vital.

In most of religious writing, "natural" religious experiences are mixed with "super," nature-defying miracles. Jesus is a good example of this. Along with his ethical teachings, we find miracles like turning water into wine (Jn 2:1-11) and healing a man blind from birth (Jn 9:1-7). Yet the Synoptic Gospels (Matthew, Mark, and Luke) record the fact that Jesus' attempts at faith-healing and exorcism did not always work and that some of the people exorcised by Jesus became re-possessed (Matthew 12:43-45, Luke 11:24-26). When Jesus was unable to heal folks in his own hometown, the Gospel of Mark (6:6 TNIV) notes that, "he was amazed at their lack of *faith*" (emphasis added), revealing him to be a "faith healer." Truly "supernatural" miracles such as Moses parting the water, Jesus walking on water, and Buddha levitating and gliding over the water are outside the experience of the modern world and have yet to be demonstrated for science. These ancient stories are better explained in two ways. The first is that of "mythic reality," meaning that they are "true but didn't happen." As metaphors, a kind of *Truth* is expressed that the miracle-worker was an extraordinary person, favored by God. Modern people who read these stories too literally and tried to replicate the "miracle" have had rude consciousness-awakening! In 1967, an attempt by a group of "hippies" to levitate the Pentagon (in Washington D. C.) resulted in dismal failure. In 1972, L. S. Rao, an Indian yogi, announced that he would walk on water; the televised event, however, showed the guru taking one step into the tank and immediately sinking to the bottom! The second explanation for miracle stories is simple fraud. An example of fraud from the Old Testament is the story of Bel and the Dragon (Dan 14:1-42); this chapter is included in the Bibles of Catholics, Orthodox, and Coptic Christians and but is relegated to the Apocrypha in the Protestant Bible. Currently, a website by Erlendur Haraldsson lists several negative and inconclusive attempts to validate whether the "god men and women" of India are fraudulent or genuine.

Conclusion

The actual words of these three prominent religious figures—Zoroaster, St. Paul, and Muhammad—reveal ample evidence for a variety of religious experiences similar to those collected by The Religious Experience Research Centre. However, the nature-defying miracles attributed to them are always embellishments of subsequent writers.

To me, the "super" miracles are superfluous. It is "super" enough that human experience of the Divine is an integral part of our human nature! It is even more "super" that modern research can be used to demonstrate the phenomenological reality of religious experience. Religion is not something in old, old books; as William James realized, "personal religion will prove itself more fundamental than either theology or ecclesiasticism."

CHAPTER 5

Religious Experience of Jesus Compatible with Modern Research

~

As a religious experience researcher for the past 20 years, I have long asserted that the religious/transpersonal/mystical experiences of Jesus related in the New Testament Gospels were no different than those of the rest of us, except in degree. While most of us feel blessed to have received the light of a lone "candle" and others describe a more impressive "incandescent bulb," Jesus perceived a "beacon"! The most consistent finding to know about all religious experiences is that they change people's lives.

Modern scholarship has devised some methods to separate myth from reality regarding Jesus. In The Five Gospels and Acts of Jesus, the Jesus Seminar attempted to uncover what is authentic about Jesus, including his mystical experiences and healings, as well as the visionary experiences of him following his death. Throughout this paper, I will site their conclusions to provide a current theological perspective.

Religious Experience and Aftermath

There are two ways to sound profound about God. One is to study religion, and the other is to have a religious experience. Jesus would have learned something of Hebrew Scripture during his Jewish childhood; later, he witnessed the inspired preaching of John the Baptist. But this secondary kind of knowledge paled in comparison to what must have been a profound spiritual experience of God that transformed his own life and, unknowingly, affected the course of history for the next 2000 years! The Jesus Seminar members were skeptical that Jesus' primary religious experience occurred at his baptism by John, but they did acknowledge that Jesus, "had visionary experiences on occasion" and they did not rule out the possibility that his "baptismal experience involved a vision of some kind." The Alister Hardy Religious Experience Research Centre (RERC) files contain ample evidence of the life-changing effects of religious experience. For example, in *The Spiritual Nature of Man*, Sir Alister Hardy sites the life-changing effects of Rev. Leslie Weatherhead's religious experience at age 19 that sealed his commitment to a life in ministry (case 385). Neuropsychiatrist Richard Bucke had a profound spiritual experience at age 35 which led him to research and write a major book on mystical experience, *Cosmic Consciousness*. Additionally, Bucke continued the path of service, becoming the head of a psychiatric hospital in London, Ontario, Canada. Mary Austin was a prolific author of the late nineteenth and early twentieth centuries who wrote about the plight of women and American Indians. In her book *Experiences Facing Death*, she not only describes her spiritual experience of the presence of God at age 5 or 6, but also that it was "the one abiding reality" of her life and that she would recall it throughout her life as a source of comfort.

In *An Introduction to Religious and Spiritual Experience*, Marianne Rankin tells the story of St. Thomas Aquinas who stopped writing theology altogether following his profound mystical experience: "He proclaimed his theology mere straw in comparison to what had been revealed to him." When people have a profound spiritual experience, they characteristically require some time to process its meaning and implications. The Gospels tell us that Jesus went into the wilderness for 40 days (which is "Bible talk" for "a long time"). Following his spiritual experience of Jesus, St. Paul spent three years in reflection before deciding how his life's work should proceed (Gal 1:18). In his book, *The Power of Now*, modern-day mystic Eckerd Tolle tells that after his spiritual experience, "For the next five months, I lived in a state of uninterrupted deep peace and bliss ... I knew, of course, that something profoundly significant had happened to me, but I didn't understand it at all." He goes on to tell how it took years of reflection and study to make sense of it.

Religious experiences are usually positive, but many are not. Jesus must quote Scripture to counter the proposals of Satan (Mt 4:1-11). The Jesus Seminar was evenly divided as to whether Jesus was tested in the wilderness. Nevertheless, 4% of the first 3,000 cases gathered by the RERC were negative, and in *Negative Spiritual Experiences*, Merete Jakobsen notes that religious "rituals are the only protection against horror and darkness of the soul." In other words, what worked for Jesus works for the rest of us. Similarly, modern people are often puzzled about who they can trust to share their profound experience. Fear of being thought mentally ill by friends or family is nothing new. When Jesus starts to preach, his family thinks he is "out of his mind, and went to restrain him" (Mk 3:21 NRSV). In *Something There*, David Hay notes a 1985 study found 40% of religious experiencers have never told anyone of their experience. In *Seeing the Invisible*, Meg Maxwell and Verena Tschulin note that, in addition to fear of being thought insane, modern spiritual experiencers often relate being rebuffed when they shared their experiences. This was especially distressing when the rejection was by their minister.

Faith Healer (Placebo Effect)

We know Jesus was a faith healer because his cures were contingent on the person's "belief" or "unbelief" (Mt 13:54-58). Also, the Gospels tell plainly that some of his exorcisms were not permanent (Mt 12:43-55). The Jesus Seminar acknowledged that Jesus was a faith healer and an exorcist and considered some of his cures genuine; of course, examples of the supernatural healing, such as Jesus' reattaching a severed ear (Lk 22: 50-51), were dismissed. Unlike the descriptions detailing the crude resuscitation techniques of Old Testament prophets Elisha and Elijah (2Kgs 4:32-35, 1Kgs 17:17-23), the Gospels do not describe Jesus' method of resuscitation of near-death experiencers (Lk 7:11-17, Mt 9:18-26, Jn 11:38-44). The Jesus Seminar did not consider any of his resuscitations genuine.

Today, there is a large body of literature demonstrating the effectiveness of the placebo effect/faith healing. In *Timeless Healing*,

Hubert Benson lists a variety of physical ailments receptive to the placebo effect. In *Irreducible Mind*, Edward Kelly and Emily Williams Kelly, et.al., devote 124 pages to psychophysiological influences, including religious practices like prayer, faith healing, and voodoo.

Separating the Super from the Natural

St. Paul is one of the few ancients who left his own first-hand account of his religious experiences. Most significantly, he describes his after-death communication with Jesus (I Cor 15:8) and states frankly that the Gospel he preaches did not come from humans but was communicated to him by Jesus from beyond the grave (Gal 1:11-12, 15-17). Paul both acknowledges and encourages the religious experiences of others (I Cor 12:8-11; 14:26-33). He describes an out-of-body experience in which he is taken to the third level of Heaven (II Cor 12:2-4). While he says that others have the ability to heal (I Cor 12:9), his letters do not tell of healings; in fact, Paul writes that he was not even able to heal himself (II Cor 12:7-9). Contrast Paul's own words with the stories about him in the Acts of the Apostles in which it is claimed that he performed miracles and even raised the dead (Acts 20:9-12)! Unfortunately, Jesus was not so lucky as to have control over the writings about him.

Transfiguration

The "transfiguration" (Mt. 17:1-8, Mk 9:2-8, Lk 9:28-36) is pregnant with theological symbolism. Nevertheless, part of modern religious experience includes reports of two or more individuals seeing an apparition of a dead person or religious figure at the same time. A 1970s study (N=434) in Los Angeles, California, USA, found 2% of the residents had reported a vision of a dead person that was part of the reality of another person.[1] In *Seeing the Invisible*, a male and female both share a vision of light and then Jesus (case 3015). *In Spiritual Encounters with Unusual Light Phenomena: Lightforms*, Mark Fox notes that 10 of his 400 cases were shared experiences, including two soldiers in Northern Ireland seeing a light that gradually took the form of the Virgin Mary (case 3008). At the transfiguration, Jesus' face, "shown like the sun and his clothes became dazzling white." In another of Mark Fox's examples, a woman reports, "suddenly I was filled with a wonderful light, and I felt my face streaming with light. My mother said afterward that she would never forget my face" (case 1160).

Psychic Ability

The Gospels relate several episodes in which Jesus exhibits psychic powers, namely, his telepathic ability with the "woman at the well" (Jn 4:4-42), and two cases of pre-cognition, one regarding the miraculous catch of fish (Lk 5:4-7) and the other, the fish with the coin in its mouth to pay the Temple tax (Mt 17:24-27). In *A Measure of Heaven*, Vince Miglorie analyzes reports (N=787) sent to the International Association of Near-Death Studies (IANDS) website of which 24% were individuals who did not have a life-threatening condition. In other words, they had religious experiences similar to a near-death experience, but they were not dead or near death. One of the after-effects reported was an increase in psychic ability. While 75.5% of the clinical death group reported the development of healing and psychic abilities, the non-life-threatening spiritual experience group reported a 61.9% increase. The existence of reported psychic abilities is not proof of psychic powers which are notoriously hard to validate. Nevertheless, Ralph Hood, Peter Hill, and Bernard Spilka note that inevitably, surveys of paranormal experience and mystical experience are highly correlated.[2]

Resurrection

Most modern liberal theologians hold with St. Paul (I Cor 15) that the resurrection of Jesus was a visionary experience (Jesus raised up by God in a spiritual body rather than a physical body). The empty tomb does not solve the dilemma, since no one saw Jesus' body rise spontaneously or be removed by others. A treasure-trove of after-death communications from ancient times to the present RERC files can be produced that resemble the appearance stories of Jesus in the Gospels, but this topic is too huge to cover here.

Conclusion

The Gospels are not "pure Jesus." Instead, they are a mixture of mythic lore and supernatural miracles, intermingled with his genuine words and religious experiences. Nevertheless, as a liberal Christian, I take comfort in the continuity of religious experience from Jesus' time to the present. Jesus knew God, and my belief is that the difference between Jesus and the rest of us is not one of difference but one of degree.

CHAPTER 6

Resurrection Appearances of Jesus as After-Death Communication

Easter is a day when Christians celebrate the resurrection of Jesus; it is an occasion much more significant than their celebration of Jesus' birth at Christmas. Resurrection literally means "rising from the dead and coming back to life." Emory University professor Luke Timothy Johnson (1998, p. 11) has gone so far as to call the resurrection the "grounding for the entire Christian life." Was Jesus raised in a spiritual body or a physical body? In most traditional Christian churches, listeners will hear of a physical, bodily resurrection; in fact, a 2005 *Newsweek* (2009) poll found that half of Americans believe in a physical resurrection. This inference is based on the stories of Easter morning in the four Gospels, which relate that Jesus' body was not in the burial tomb when Mary Magdalene (present in all Gospel accounts), accompanied by one or more women (in other Gospel accounts), arrived there. This view has been perpetuated by millions of Christians since the fourth century who learned to recite from the Apostle's Creed the phrase, " ... resurrection of the body and life everlasting." Interestingly, the same 2005 Newsweek poll (2009) showed one-third of Americans think that

Jesus' resurrection was a spiritual one! My purpose is to present this view as the authentic one, first, because it is more consistent with the New Testament accounts, and second, because it is most compatible with scientific research into spiritually transformative experiences over the past 125 years. As a religious experience researcher myself, I am convinced that mystical religious experiences are a normal part of a healthy, non-psychotic human life and that the religious experiences of Jesus represent the same phenomena as those of all people, despite time or culture.

In the early twentieth century, philosopher and psychical researcher James Hyslop (1908, p. 383) and theologian Rudolph Otto (1950, pp. 222–229) began to see the resurrection of Jesus as a visionary/spiritual experience—what is now called an after-death communication (ADC). More recently, liberal theologians (Funk & the Jesus Seminar, 1998, pp. 449–495) and religious experience researchers (Wiebe, 1997, pp. 106–107; 121; 212–222) have favored a spiritual resurrection over a physical resurrection.

"An after-death communication (ADC) is a spiritual experience that occurs when someone is connected directly and spontaneously by a deceased family member or friend" (Guggenheim & Guggenheim, 1996, p 15). Guggenheim and Guggenheim (1996) acknowledged that Jesus and his mother Mary are the best-known ADCs but elected not to make the comparison for fear of offending Christians (p. 11). Obviously, I have included Jesus, his mother Mary, and other divine beings, as that is the purpose of this paper.

In the New Testament, Paul has the distinction of being the earliest writer, as well as the only writer to give a first-person account of Jesus' resurrection. Paul's ADC with Jesus occurred about four years after Jesus' death, and he wrote about this experience about 20 years later (White, 2004, pp. 150, 172). Paul was not a follower during Jesus' lifetime but became one of the most influential Apostles, having enormous influence over the direction of early Christianity, especially in the West. Paul's letters also provide the only verified second-hand reports of the resurrection—those of Peter, an early disciple of Jesus, and James, the brother of Jesus, whom Paul had met. These are Paul's own words: "He (Jesus) appeared to Cephas (Peter) and to the Twelve. Then he appeared to more than 500 brothers and sisters at one time, most of whom are still alive, though some have died. Then he appeared to James, then to all the Apostles. Last of all, as one untimely born, he appeared also to me." (I Cor 15:5–8 NRSV) About 80 years after the death of Jesus

(White, 2004, p. 252), Luke—widely accepted to be the author of the Acts of the Apostles—tried to suggest that Paul's experience of Jesus was somehow different from the appearances of Jesus to his former earthly companions. Luke clearly explained that he was a compiler of stories that were handed down to him (Lk 1:1–3). Luke's accounts of Jesus appearing to Paul in the Acts of the Apostles (Acts 9:3–9; 22:4–16; 26:9–18) are somewhat contradictory, but in all three accounts Paul saw a "light from heaven" and heard the voice of Jesus. Although this experience sounds like a modern ADC (Fox, 2008, p 41–43), it does not square with Paul's own first-person account that (a) he had "seen Jesus our Lord" (I Cor 9:1 NRSV), (b) "God ... was pleased to reveal his Son to me" (Gal 1:15–16), and (c) "he [Jesus] appeared also to me" (I Cor 15:8b). Paul stated definitely that his ADC from Jesus was identical to that of the others (I Cor 15:5–8 NRSV). Paul was equally adamant that resurrected bodies are spiritual in nature: "It is sown in a physical body, it is raised a spiritual body" (I Cor 15:44 NRSV). He emphasized the point that "flesh and blood cannot inherit the Kingdom of God nor does the perishable inherit the imperishable" (I Cor 15:50 NRSV). In other words, Paul knew nothing about a physical resurrection of Jesus. Many years after Paul's letters were written, the writers of the Gospels implied a physical resurrection of Jesus because of the empty tomb. In reality, the empty tomb adds nothing (Funk et al., 1998, p. 463), as no one saw Jesus revive and walk out of the tomb, and no one saw anyone remove Jesus' body as was later claimed (Matt 28:11–15).

The *First Letter of Peter,* written about 50–65 years after Jesus' death under the name of Peter (White, 2004, p. 274), also presents a spiritual resurrection. It states: "He [Christ] was put to death in the flesh but made alive in the Spirit" (I Peter 3:18b NRSV).

The Gospel of Mark is the earliest, written about 40–45 years after Jesus' death (White, 2004, p. 233). Its original ending had no resurrection appearances but ended with the mystery of an empty tomb.

Much later, resurrection stories were added to Mark that appear to be a synopsis of those in the other three Gospels (Funk et al., 1998, pp. 465–467).

The Gospel of Matthew, written 50–60 years after the death of Jesus (White, 2004, p. 244), has a pre-resurrection story at the time of Jesus' death stating that "the tombs also were opened, and many bodies of the saints who had fallen asleep were raised. After his resurrection they came out of the tombs and entered the holy city and appeared to many" (Matt 27:52–53 NRSV). The writer of Matthew had Jesus appear first to

Mary Magdalene and the "other Mary" who took hold of his feet and worshiped him. The second ADC of Jesus was placed in Galilee where he appeared to his 11 disciples: "When they saw him, they worshipped him; but some doubted" (Matt 28:9–10, 17 NRSV).

The Gospel of Luke, written 60-70 years after the death of Jesus (White, 2004, p. 252), told of two of Jesus' Apostles meeting Jesus while walking on the road to Emmaus. Luke said that their "eyes were kept from recognizing him." After talking to Jesus and inviting him to supper, he broke bread, they recognized him, and he vanished from their sight. Later he appeared to the Apostles and asked them to touch him. Luke reported that Jesus stood among the disciples suddenly, saying, "Peace be with you," and the disciples were startled and terrified and "thought they were seeing a ghost." Then he ate a piece of fish (Lk 24).

The Gospel of John, written 65-90 years after the death of Jesus (White, 2004, p. 310), includes many other appearance stories. When Jesus appeared to Mary Magdalene, she did not recognize him until he spoke her name. Unlike the Gospel of Matthew in which Mary Magdalene touched Jesus, Jesus told Mary not to touch him. Jesus later appeared suddenly in a locked room to all the Apostles but Thomas. Because Thomas doubted their story, Jesus appeared again to the Apostles while Thomas was present and asked Thomas to touch the wound in his side. Later, Jesus appeared to seven Apostles who were fishing in the Sea of Tiberias; they hadn't caught anything, and Jesus—using his psychic ability—told them where to cast their nets. They then recognized him, and Jesus served them fish and bread (Jn 20;21).

The Acts of the Apostles was written 80 years after Jesus' death (White, 2004, p. 252). It states that Jesus appeared to people for 40 days, after which he ascended to Heaven on the Day of Pentecost (Acts 1). (This is curious because there is a previous Ascension story in Luke [Lk 24:50–53].) What is the purpose of placing the Ascension story 40 days after Easter, if Jesus was raised up to God on Easter Day? A problem exists only for those advocating a "physical body" scenario. Using Paul's view—which is the modern view—that Jesus' resurrection was an ADC, no explanation is needed because spiritual beings can appear at will from the afterlife whether the percipient is an ancient who viewed heaven as "above the earth" or a modern who views heaven as "another reality."

In summary, I have identified nine categories of Jesus' resurrection appearances in the accounts of the New Testament:

1. He appeared to individuals.
2. He appeared to small groups and large groups.
3. Sometimes Jesus' former friends did not recognize him.
4. Sometimes people touched Jesus.
5. In one account, Mary Magdalene was asked not to touch Jesus.
6. Jesus appeared and disappeared instantly; he walked through locked doors.
7. Jesus broke bread, served breakfast, and ate!
8. Jesus used his psychic powers—to predict where to catch fish.
9. Jesus converted people (like St. Paul).

All of these behaviors exhibited by the resurrected Jesus have been reported throughout history. Turning now to modern accounts of after death appearances of Jesus, other divine figures, and ordinary people, such accounts demonstrate that all of the above nine behaviors exhibited in the New Testament are present in modern-day accounts by non-psychotic individuals and verified by modern religious experience researchers.

1. Individuals. The following is a twentieth century account by a British woman: "All at once I felt someone near me, a Presence entered this little room of which I became immediately conscious. This feeling or second sense could be very frightening, but I was not afraid or alarmed. I saw in my mind our Blessed Saviour, and the picture of Him has never left me." (Maxwell & Tschudin, 2005, p. 115)

2. Small and large groups. Post-death visions seen by more than one person—whether the vision is a religious figure or an ordinary person—are well-documented (Guggenheim & Guggenheim, 1996, pp. 285–300; Kalish & Reynolds, 1973; Myers, 1903, pp. 62–65; Wiebe, 1997, pp. 15–88). In a study of 434 residents of Los Angeles, including persons of Black, European, Japanese, and Mexican origins, "slightly over 2% reported post-death encounters that were part of the reality of another person present at the time" (Kalish & Reynolds, 1973, p.219). In a study of 400 mystical experiences that involved light, 2.5% involved multiple witnesses (Fox, 2008, p. 64).

In the following account, a woman and her husband-to-be shared a vision of Jesus while they were walking in the moonlight: "Then the figure emerged, a most brilliant sight. We were both speechless, but not afraid, it was so beautiful. The figure, Jesus Christ, glided onto the centre of the road while we were on rough pavement. . . We still remember every detail, but our views on religion have deepened; although, still, we are not too religious." (Maxwell & Tschudin, 2005, pp. 77–78)

3. Not recognized. On the Road to Emmaus, "their eyes were kept from recognizing him" (Lk 24:16). Modern people have also experienced visions of Jesus in disguise (Migliore, 2009, pp. 137–139).
The following is a woman's vision of Jesus while she was meditating: "I went forward, alone, toward an old man who stood at the very end of the rose-covered arches. I stopped before him. He asked me if ministry was what I really wanted. I replied affirmatively. He then used his thumb to make the sign of the cross on my forehead, my hands, my feet, my lips, and over my heart—in that order. Then he said, 'Go in peace.' I wondered who he was. He looked at me with sad eyes and said, 'Don't you know me?' With his words, the illusion of the old man fell away, and I realized that he was Christ" (Sparrow, 1995, pp. 150–151).

4. Touching. In one account, a woman touches Jesus' hair (Sparrow, 1995, p. 32). Ordinary people also come back from the dead, and their loved ones report having touched them: "After the sudden death of my husband about nine years ago, I had several experiences, which proved to me that there is a life after death. I am not a Spiritualist, nor a Churchgoer, but I try to follow Jesus, and I am a great believer in meditation, as a way to God. After his passing, I both saw and spoke to my husband and held his hand. This hand was strong and not at all ghost-like, nor was his appearance. I was alone at the time, so no medium there to act as a link. Probably this is not a detail to prove God's existence, but to me, it indeed did." (Hardy, 1997, p. 47) John Hick (2006, p. 34) noted that other holy figures have appeared to their followers and provided an account of a young Hindu embracing Lord Krishna. In a study of 293 widows and widowers, Dewi Rees found not only that slightly less than half of them had contact with their deceased spouse but also that 2.7% actually touched them (Fenwick & Fenwick, 2008, p. 121).

5. Not touching. This next modern visionary account is of a woman's dead husband: "Not long afterwards, I awoke shaking violently from head to foot. He had appeared to me, radiant, smiling, his usual happy self. I had impulsively gone forward to greet him, saying, 'Do you know—I've just been having a dream.' Something stopped me before I touched him— he was there, completely himself, but of a different 'substance.' I drew back, as it were, looking in through a frame, to another dimension. I stopped, and said to him, 'I know, I understand.' This experience, following his death, has given me great comfort ... " (Hardy, 1997, p. 47).

6. Vanishing, reappearing, walking through solids. Modern visions of Jesus include his appearance to Charles Finney, a nineteenth century minister: "There was no fire or light in the room; nevertheless, it appeared as if it were perfectly light. As I went in and shut the door, it seemed as if I met the Lord Jesus Christ face to face. It did not occur to me that it was a wholly mental state; it seemed that I saw him as I would see any other man." (Bucke, 1991, p. 288)

7. Food. In *Visions of Jesus*, Phillip Wiebe (1997, p. 43) recounted a modern story of Jesus offering wine.

In his book, *Long March to Freedom*, Tom Hargrove (1995, pp. 277, 334) described his experience of being held captive by the FARC in Colombia. In the book, Tom briefly described his vision of Jesus, and he was kind enough to send me an expanded account of this encounter:

> "Terribly depressed, I went to El Templo on May 26. Alone by my broken cross of bamboo, I started to cry. Then something strange happened. Was it a religious experience or a hunger-induced hallucination? I don't know. But I thought I saw an ephemeral, bearded man walking from the woods to El Templo. I described him in my diary as having a Kris Kristofferson beard, and wearing jeans, red plaid flannel shirt, high leather boots—the lace-up kind. The man came closer, and his face seemed exactly that of the stereotyped Jesus whose portrait hangs on Sunday School walls. He laughed, and told me to sit on a log. I'm sorry I was crying, I said. 'You can cry here whenever you wish,' the man replied. Then somehow, he opened a liter bottle of Gallo Hearty Burgundy and poured two crystal goblets of red wine. We drank, then he said he must leave, but maybe we could visit again. He added (I wrote in my diary), but I might include him more when I'm having fun after I leave here. That ephemeral man walked back into the forest, and I was alone again. I had never before and have never again had such an experience. What made it still stranger was (that) I have never remotely thought of Jesus dressed in jeans, red flannel shirt, and lumber-jack boots." (Tom Hargrove, personal communication, August 23, 2002)

When I questioned Tom, he said, "If Jesus had been dressed in robes and sandals, I would be less inclined to think it's real. It's the only story that I have a hard time telling. It didn't change me, but it sure enough impressed me. I guess it did make a big difference to me." (Tom Hargrove, personal communication, August 23, 2002)

8. Psychic powers. In this example, Jesus' Mother Mary also appears to have had psychic powers. After giving a talk on the scientific study of the paranormal a few years ago, a colleague (personal communication, October 31, 2001) came to tell me of her grandmother's vision of the Virgin Mary. In Galveston's Hurricane of 1900, her grandmother's family fled to the third floor of their house as the water rose almost to that level. Her grandmother prayed the rosary, and the Virgin Mary appeared to her and told her they would be spared. The water then began to recede.

9. Conversions (like Paul's). According to one account, a Jew had an encounter with Jesus, after which he converted to Christianity and went on to become a bishop (Rankin, 2008, pp. 101-102). A modern account involves an atheist who saw Jesus and then became a believing Christian (Maxwell & Tschudin, 2005, pp. 104-105). Mark Fox (2008, pp. 41-42) cited a Hindu who had a vision of Jesus and then converted to Christianity.

The following account is from a woman who was worried about the fate of her dead brother because he had not become a Christian. Five months after his death, she reported: "I looked up off to my right, my brother was there with the Lord! They were life-sized very very real, very solid and distinct and three-dimensional. They were very close, shoulder-to-shoulder, and I only saw the upper portion of them. Leon (her brother) was facing me, the Lord was wearing a robe and facing him, and they were both smiling. My brother appeared younger than when he died and looked very healthy. Nothing needed to be said— Leon was with the Lord and that's all I wanted to know." (Guggenheim & Guggenheim, 1996, p. 309) This story echoes the great Universalist passage, "And I, when I am lifted up from the earth, will draw all people to myself. " (Jn 12:32).

Veridical Cases

The validity of an ADC is greatly enhanced when the experience can be verified by others. These "veridical" cases of mystical religious experiences occur when more than one person sees the vision at the same time or when the vision imparts information that would not or could not have been known to the person who experienced the vision (Fox, 2008, pp. 57–77; Maxwell & Tschudin, 2005, p. 78; Myers, 1903, pp. 40–42).

Aftereffects

To me, the most impressive aftereffect of any mystical/religious/spiritual experience, including ADCs, is how they have changed people's lives for the better (Hardy, 1997, pp. 101-103; Hay, 1987, p.157; Hick, 2006, pp. 51, 206; Maxwell & Tschudin, 2005, pp. 36-44; Yao & Badham, 2007, p. 45). Mother Teresa heard the voice of Jesus asking her to serve the poor in India (Rankin, 2008, p. 206). When Martin Luther King was wavering about his commitment to the civil rights movement, he heard the voice of Jesus giving him reassurance and courage to go on (Marsh, 2005).

The next two twentieth-century accounts are from David Parke, a Unitarian Universalist minister. The first occurred after his wife had a stillborn child: "Late at night, under a soft October rain, a Christ-like presence entered my life that night as if to say, 'David, your baby is with God, and you and your bride will recover from this loss, and you will become parents again.' In faith, I saw in my mind's eye my unborn son rising on a sunbeam to Heaven. I never doubted that God in Christ came to me and spoke to me that night." (David Parke, personal communication, January 22, 2010) His second experience took place the following year when he was a young divinity student at the University of Chicago: "Then mid-way through my first year, the crucified Christ appeared to me in my dormitory room. For those few moments—I do not know for how long—Jesus Christ crucified occupied my entire personal horizon.

His tragic visage and piercing eyes penetrated to the bottom of my soul. He did not speak. I did not speak. Although unspoken, the message was clear—'I come from the God of Abraham, Isaac, and Jacob. Your life is your own, but it is also God's. Do not be diverted by self-indulgence and concern for the opinions of others. You are called to minister—and to minister is to suffer as I have suffered. Give yourself to those who come to you in brokenness. Listen to them. Heal them. Love them. You can do less, but more than this you cannot do. I am with you always.' You will understand, friends, that other than my own birth and the birth of my children, this was the most important moment of my life." (David Parke, personal communication, January 22, 2010)

Conclusion

Based on the evidence of modern accounts of ADCs of Jesus, other divine beings, and ordinary people, it is apparent that the resurrection appearances of Jesus in the Gospels resemble the modern ones.

Modern liberal biblical scholars, such as the Jesus Seminar, see the empty tomb story as a later development (Funk et al., 1998, p. 462).

Recent scholarship into spiritually transformative experiences— including ADCs—indicates that they are quite common in the general population in the U.S., Europe, and China (Argyle, 2000, pp. 47–59; Fenwick & Fenwick, 2008, pp. 120-121; Yao & Badham, 2007, pp. 184-192). Although ordinary people appear to their loved ones— usually only one or two—Jesus has continued to appear throughout the ages both to those who love him and to others. Although ADCs of Jesus, other divine figures, and ordinary people—both ancient and modern— do not prove afterlife, they definitely point to it and show a continuity of experience that is part of the phenomenological reality of humanity. This phenomenon is a source of great comfort to me, and I hope it is to other people who are skeptical of a physical resurrection.

CHAPTER 7

Resurrection Appearances of Jesus as After-Death Communication: Rejoinder to Gary Habermas

∿

G ary Habermas was correct in stating that he and I agree that Jesus was raised from the dead and that there is a substantial amount of data from religious experience research that points to an afterlife (Habermas, 2012). He acknowledged that scholars before me have suggested that Jesus' post-resurrection appearances might be interpreted as a variation of after-death communications (ADCs), also known as post-death visions. Although he affirmed the similarities between Jesus' post-resurrection appearances and modern-day ADCs, he was adamant that they are not the same. I believe that Habermas' theological roots prevented him from accepting anything but a resurrected Jesus with a physical body, returned to Earth in a supernatural miracle, unique among other holy figures or ordinary people. As I have maintained in previous writings, "Truly supernatural miracles such as Moses parting the water, Jesus walking on water, and Buddha levitating and gliding over the water are outside the experience of the modern world and yet to be demonstrated by science" (Vincent, 2007, p. 7), but religious experience is as common today as it was in ancient times.

Some time after the editor of this Journal submitted my article to Habermas for his review and he agreed to write a response, he and I spoke on the telephone at length (personal communication, July 12, 2012). I was pleasantly surprised to learn that he had some knowledge of the growing amount of data on transpersonal experiences being mined in the fields of social science and medicine. However, in his References, he cited only two religious experience researchers: Michael Perry and myself (Habermas, 2012).

My article was intentionally based on research into spiritually transformative experiences (mystical experiences, deathbed visions, near-death experiences, ADCs) as integral to the normal, healthy human life experience. Habermas (2012) faulted me for ignoring "historians, philosophers, and New Testament researchers" (p. 151) and chose to frame his arguments in theological terms. However, my paper dealt with the universality of religious experience across time and culture, and any reference to philosophy or theology was only tangential. For me, theology is basically an argument about a book— or, in the case of the vast Hindu scriptures, a set of books. In my view, spiritually transformative experience is the basis for all that is holy in scripture, and the validity of the Bible or any other sacred book rests on the religious experience(s) in it. I share the view of William James that religious experience is primary, and religion is secondary (James, 1902/1990, p. 35).

My doctorate is in counseling psychology, and I am a religious experience researcher; I use the older term "religious" because the topic of my original article is the resurrection. Many of my colleagues prefer to use the word "spiritual" rather than "religious." I am not quite as hostile to the idea of religion as Raymond Moody (2012) who stated that "notions of afterlife can exist independent of religion. In fact, I can now say with assurance that 'religion' and 'afterlife' are two entirely different concepts linked together only by religious dogma" (p. 32). Sir Alister Hardy (1997), founder of the Religious Experience Research Centre, asserted that religious experience is not supernatural but rather is part of normal reality (pp. 131–142). Some time ago, I began reading scientific literature exploring the ADC phenomenon in which Jesus has appeared to modern people. More importantly, I began paying special attention to the first-hand accounts of people I knew to be credible and not psychotic. When I reexamined the stories of Jesus' resurrection in the New Testament, I was delighted to find that they resembled modern ADCs (Vincent, 2012).

Habermas's (2012) "Response" began with some "forceful reasons" (p. 149) that Jesus' post-resurrection appearances are different from ADCs before he presented his "six major dissimilarities" (p. 153) between Jesus' post-resurrection appearances and contemporary ADCs. I will now try to provide some clarity. Habermas took issue with my using L. Michael White (2004) for references in dating the gospels. Granted, conservative scholars tend to prefer the earliest dates possible for New Testament writers and liberal scholars generally use later dates, but I did not choose White to "favor my conclusions" (Habermas, 2012, p. 151). I did so for economy; White has used broader time spans, and I find White to be a generally fair source. The 10-year discrepancy in dates is irrelevant to my case; even the earlier date of 60CE is 30 years after Jesus' death and provides plenty of time for myth-making to begin.

Habermas (2012) cited my assertion that Paul's first-hand and second-hand accounts (I Cor 15:4–8) of Jesus being raised in a spiritual body offer more credibility than the later Gospel writers' reports of an empty tomb that implies a bodily resurrection. Sociologist and religious experience researcher James McClenon (2002, p. 116) classified experience as first-hand, second-hand, and folkloric (greater than second-hand). By this standard, most of the Bible is folklore. Many religious experience researchers and liberal Christian scholars (Funk & the Jesus Seminar, 1998, pp. 449–495) took I Corinthians 15 as the only reliable information about Jesus' resurrection.

In addition, Habermas (2012) took issue with my assertion that Paul's view of a spiritual resurrection is an ADC. He claimed that what I call the "modern view" is actually out-of-date. It is most decidedly not out-of-date with religious experience researchers and liberal Christian scholars such as G. Riley (2001, pp. 154-156), J. Tabor (2006, pp. 230-238, 329-330), W. E. Phipps (2008, pp. 188-210), P. Wiebe (1997, pp. 121-125), J. Hick (2008, pp. 88-95), A. F. Segal (2004, pp. 393, 403-440, 448), J. McClenon (1994, pp. 75-77), J. H. Ellens (2008, p. 159), M. Borg (1997, pp. 92-93), and T. Harpur (2011, pp. 131–156).

Finally, the Jesus Seminar, a group of liberal scholars intent on separating the authentic words of Jesus from the mythic parts of the Gospels, focused in 1995 on Jesus' resurrection. "More than 90% of the Fellows and a huge majority of the Associates, agreed that Jesus' resurrection did not involve the resuscitation of a corpse" (Scott, 2008,

p. 45) and that his body decayed in the usual way. In my mind, this conclusion puts them in agreement with Paul who clearly stated, "What is sown is perishable, what is raised is imperishable" (I Cor 15:42 NRSV).

Habermas's (2012) point on the translation of John 20:17 is well taken. He stated that new translations have Jesus telling Mary Magdalene not to "hold on" to him rather than to "touch" him. However, this variant in translation does not alter my assertion that the resurrection was a spiritual experience. Modern ADCs sometimes include an aspect of touch between the living and the deceased. In my view, Habermas (2012) grasped at straws when he cited an obscure point of logic that things can appear similar but not be the same. With this point, he seemed to exclude the possibility that things that appear similar could be the same. In asserting that Jesus' resurrection was unique among all others, Habermas's position flies in the face of the larger truth of Occam's Razor that favors the simplest explanation: Jesus' post-resurrection appearances resemble modern-day ADCs, and so they are. Science is based on observation, and Habermas's argument for exceptionalism in the case of Jesus defies common sense.

Habermas's (2012) survey of scholars who support his view is countered by an exceptionally large number of scholars who favor my position—the largest group being the Jesus Seminar. Their analysis of the true words and deeds of Jesus remains a major piece of scholarship (Funk, Hoover, & the Jesus Seminar, 1993; Funk & the Jesus Seminar, 1998). More importantly, new cases of ADCs are continuously being added to databases in departments of social science and medicine in universities and medical schools. Erlendur Haraldsson's (2012) latest book, *The Departed Among the Living*, is an excellent example that chronicles 449 cases in Iceland.

Habermas began his "Six Major Dissimilarities" with his defense of the empty tomb.

1. Personally, I prefer to leave the question of the empty tomb a mystery, as an empty tomb is simply unnecessary for Jesus' spiritual resurrection (Vincent, 2012). The Jesus Seminar felt that the empty tomb represented a later development (Funk & the Jesus Seminar, 1998, p. 462). In "Brand X Easters," Robert Price (2008) noted that the original Gospel of Mark has no resurrection story but ends with the empty tomb. Price also stated that many ancient Hellenistic texts have a missing body and an

assurance from a heavenly voice or visitor that the person has been taken to heaven; he asserted that this is enough evidence to indicate an ascension (Scott, 2008, pp 49-53). Price's examples include Herakles, Romulus, and Apollonius of Tyana. Space does not allow me to explore all the possible explanations for the empty tomb, but it is worth noting that James Tabor (2006, pp.233–240, 319–330) gave several explanations for the empty tomb and proposed his own theory that Jesus was re-buried in a family tomb.

2. Habermas contended that Jesus predicted his own death, unlike cases of modern ADCs. However, the text in Matthew states that at Jesus' death, "the tombs also were opened, and many bodies of the saints who had fallen asleep were raised. After his resurrection they came out of the tombs and entered the holy city and appeared to many" (Matt 27:52–53 NRSV). These were clearly spiritual resurrections, as the bodies of these long-dead saints would have been thoroughly decomposed. Jesus himself anticipated a spiritual resurrection when he proclaimed that at death people become "like angels in heaven" (Matt 22:30, Mk 12:25, Lk 20:36). According to the Jesus Seminar, Jesus' predictions of his own death were put on his lips after the fact (Mk 8:31, 9:31, 10:33-34; Funk et al., 1993, pp. 78, 83, 94). But is the Jesus Seminar correct in this incidence? Mystical experiences of God and psychic ability go hand-in-hand, and Jesus is no exception (Vincent, 2010, p. 12). Premonitions were 7% of the first 3,000 cases gathered by Sir Alister Hardy, founder of the Religious Experience Research Centre (Hardy, 1997, pp. 26, 45-6). Ordinary people sometimes have premonitions of their own death; Abraham Lincoln is a famous example (Moody, 1994, pp. 3-4). The problem with the New Testament or any other holy book is determining what is factual and what is later myth-making. Modern cases of ordinary people's religious/ mystical experiences enhance the credibility of ancient accounts.

3. Habermas said that the ancients were aware that Jesus' resurrection appearances were somehow different from other ADCs. Crossan (1998, pp. xiii–xxxi) refuted this point by arguing that Paul's Greco- Roman audience would have had no problem with Jesus' resurrection because it fit well with their conception of the behavior of gods, heroes, and dead humans.

4. Habermas stated that, according to the New Testament, Jesus made multiple post-resurrection appearances, and that such multiplicity

is unlike the ADCs of ordinary individuals. I would add—more profoundly—that modern ADCs with Jesus indicate that Jesus' resurrection is still in progress (Vincent, 2012)! Jesus' mother Mary, who was declared the "Queen of Heaven" by Pope Pius XII (Phipps, 2008, pp. 50-51), is considered by comparative religion scholars to be a goddess in her own right. Apparitions of Mary to multiple witnesses are well-documented, including 14 people at Knock, Ireland in 1879 (Fox, 2008, pp. 39-40); most famously, Mary appeared to 70,000 people who witnessed a unique celestial event at Fatima, Portugal in 1917 (Sparrow, 2002, pp. 125-126). It is worth mentioning that divine beings from other religions such as Lord Krishna (Hick, 2006, p. 34), Amitabha, and Guanyin (Yao & Badham, 2007, pp. 5, 38), also appear to modern people. In ADCs, ordinary people usually have no need to appear to anyone other than their loved ones. In *Hello From Heaven*, Bill Guggenheim and Judy Guggenheim (1995) reported instances of ADCs of ordinary people who reappear many years later (p. 259-274), who sometimes appeared to help loved ones recover lost objects or money (p. 275-290), who appeared to protect their families from harm (p. 290-306), who appeared to prevent suicide (p. 307-322), and who occasionally appear to two or more people (p. 323-340). Divine Beings have a greater number of people who love them; therefore, they have a greater need to comfort, warn, assure, and save their followers and other souls. The phenomenology of the ADCs is the same for ordinary people and Divine Beings, whether the occurrence is ancient or modern.

5. Habermas returned to the idea that Luke's description of Paul's experience of Jesus in the Acts of the Apostles—written many years later by an author who admitted he was not an eye-witness—is somehow more accurate than Paul's first-hand account. Luke discounted Paul's own account (Phipps, 2008, p. 256; Vincent, 2012). Contrary to Habermas's assertion that light is foreign to ADCs, it occasionally appears in ADC accounts (Fox, 2008, p. 51). More relevant is the fact that Paul himself did not mention light in his own descriptive writing of his religious experience of Jesus (I Cor 15:4-8).

6. Habermas claimed that the majority of modern scholars accept the resurrection of Jesus as a bodily event. This is not remarkable. I am certain that a return to second century Egypt—at a time when the ancient Egyptian religion was being threatened by the spread of various Greco-Roman religions and Christianity—would find a majority of

Egyptian priests voting "yes" on the physical resurrection of Osiris and his subsequent elevation to King of the Dead (Mojsov, 2005, pp. 38-53, 111-119).

At the beginning of my original paper, I stated that my view of Jesus' resurrection in a spiritual body is favored by liberal theologians and, more importantly, by religious experience researchers. I contended that the differences between Jesus' post-resurrection appearances—as well as Jesus' initial mystical experience of God—and those transpersonal experiences of others are not one of kind but of degree (Vincent, 2010a). In conclusion to this dialog with Habermas, I persist in that contention. Thanks to religious experience research over the past 150 years, including mystical/spiritual experiences, near-death experiences, death-bed visions, and ADCs, humanity currently knows more about how we experience God and afterlife than we have known at any other time in recorded history (Vincent, 2010b, 2011).

CHAPTER 8

Religious Experience Research Reveals Universalist Principles

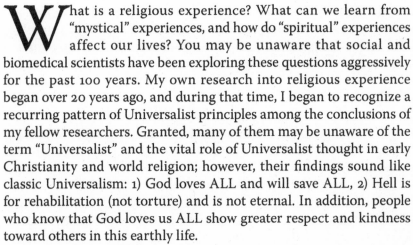

W hat is a religious experience? What can we learn from "mystical" experiences, and how do "spiritual" experiences affect our lives? You may be unaware that social and biomedical scientists have been exploring these questions aggressively for the past 100 years. My own research into religious experience began over 20 years ago, and during that time, I began to recognize a recurring pattern of Universalist principles among the conclusions of my fellow researchers. Granted, many of them may be unaware of the term "Universalist" and the vital role of Universalist thought in early Christianity and world religion; however, their findings sound like classic Universalism: 1) God loves ALL and will save ALL, 2) Hell is for rehabilitation (not torture) and is not eternal. In addition, people who know that God loves us ALL show greater respect and kindness toward others in this earthly life.

Research into religious experiences can be and is conducted using the same criteria that is used to investigate any other psychological phenomena. These include:

1. Case studies of transpersonal experience.
2. Sociological surveys that tell who and what percentage of the population have religious experiences.
3. Psychological tests that measure not only the mental health of the individual but also evaluate the depth of mystical experiences.
4. Biomedical and neuroscience testing, including, in some cases, the EEG, PET-scan, and fMRI to document genuine altered states of consciousness and demonstrate that mystical experiences are not just wishful thinking; EEGs and EKGs that allow us to document death in Near-Death Experiences (NDEs) that occur in hospitals.
5. Sociological and psychological investigations that assess the after-effects these experiences have on people.
6. Controlled experimental research (such as Panke's experiment testing psychedelics).

Religious or spiritual experiences relate to the direct experience of the Holy Spirit of God (or if you prefer, Ultimate Reality). According to David Hay, former head of the Religious Experience Research Centre, both terms describe the same phenomena, but "religious" experience is preferred by people who attend church and "spiritual" experience is favored by people who don't. I also include those religious experiences that point to life after death, namely near-death experiences, deathbed visions, and after-death communications. The following is a sampling of 22 religious experience researchers whose conclusions can reinforce our confidence in the validity and truth of our Universalist message:

God Loves ALL and Will Save ALL.

Bill and Judy Guggenheim research after-death communications. These usually occur when a loved-one comes back to tell you they are all right, but it also includes experiences with religious figures such as Jesus appearing to Paul (I Cor 15) and modern people. In their book *Hello From Heaven* they unequivocally state, "no one regardless of cruelty of malicious crimes he or she may have committed on earth is ever forgotten or forsaken." They go on to state that the criterion for healing seems to be admission of responsibility for the hurt, pain, and suffering they have caused others.

One of the most thoughtful and prolific near-death researchers is social psychologist Ken Ring. In his most recent book with Evelyn Valarino *Lessons from the Light*, he reiterates his absolute certainty that everyone will come to the light. He tells the story of a person sexually abused by her father who, when asked if Adolf Hitler would eventually come into the light, and she said, "Yes." Later she said, "Even my father will see the light." In an earlier book, *Heading Toward Omega*, Prof. Ring states, "Indeed, the strongest evidence of the NDErs' universalistically spiritual orientation and in many ways the culmination of the qualities already discussed is their belief in the underlying unity of all religions and their desire for a universal religious faith that will transcend the historical divisiveness of the world's great religions."

Richard Bucke, a Canadian neuro-psychiatrist and comparative religion scholar, saw a unity of all religions and people. His Universalist perspectives came to him in a powerful mystical experience and lead him to research and write the book, *Cosmic Consciousness*.

The philosopher Mark Webb notes in his article, "Religious Experience as Doubt Resolution," that "nearly all religious experiences result in the belief that the universe is an essentially friendly place; that is, that we shouldn't worry about the future. People who have had experiences of this sort tend to live more calmly than others, having acquired a strong feeling that the world is essentially just and that they particularly are 'cared for.' This is true even of those experiences that include a conviction that the world is fallen and sinful, because they also include a conviction that God is sovereign and loves his creatures.

The second area agreement is that all humans are closely interrelated in some way ... the pragmatic value of these two results is clear: people who believe these propositions will tend to be happier and more concerned about each other. The Presbyterian minister and theologian J. Harold Ellens writes in his book *Understanding Religious Experience* that he personally has had at least a dozen such religious experiences. He states that, "God has declared God's covenant of unconditional and universal grace to all people, guaranteeing that we are all God's people and God is our God, no matter what." Rev. Ellens is a committed Universalist who was once accused of heresy by an elder for preaching Universalism and subsequently brought before trial by the Presbyterian hierarchy where the charges were eventually dismissed.

Journalist, near-death researcher, and former Anglican priest Tom Harpur was a committed Universalist. In his book *Life After Death*, he states, "If we truly believe in an all-loving gracious Source of all things, the kind of accepting presence imaged by the father in the Parable of the Prodigal Son, then it seems to me to be utterly incongruous to hold that anyone will be lost. We are all God's off-spring or children as New

Testament Christianity—and most other religions—makes clear ... I fail to see how heaven or eternal life would be bliss of any kind unless one were assured that all will be sharers in it. At this ultimate family occasion, there will finally be no empty chairs, no missing faces."

Religious experience researcher Nona Coxhead in her book *The Relevance of Bliss* states, "for just as the sun shines on everyone without discrimination, the realization that love and light will be fully accessible to all of us following our bodily demise is a message of joy that those who have returned from 'the gates of death' bring us."

Religious experience researchers Meg Maxwell and Verena Tschudin, in their book, *Seeing the Invisible*, note, "The most striking element of the personal experiences in the collection of the Religious Experience Research Centre is that they are overwhelmingly positive in nature. They enhance and enrich life; they point forward; they are positive; they are benign."

The great Universalist/pluralist philosopher John Hick acknowledges that he has had several mystical experiences. In his book *The Fifth Dimension*, he notes that what we know from mysticism is that, "if our big picture is basically correct, nothing good that has been created in human life will ever be lost...this is not a faith wherein no harm can befall us in this present life, or those we love, but a faith that ultimately, in Lady Julian's words (Julian of Norwich), 'All shall be well, and all shall be well, and all manner of things shall be well.'"

Paul Robb, author of *The Kindness of God*, a book that is a collection of religious experiences, notes, "If there is a single message in the accounts of this book, I believe it is this: God loves us all without exception. No matter how black the soul, the soul is still loved. I believe God's love is like sunlight. The sun gives off light; it is incapable of giving off darkness. God gives off love; he is incapable of giving off anger or hatred or vengeance or jealousy or punishment. The themes of God's love, and His kindness, occur again and again in the accounts in this book and at the Religious Experience Research Centre."

Hell Is for Instruction and Is Not Permanent

The first near-death experience I ever read was that of the psychiatrist George Ritchie. Dr. Richie happens to be the professor who trained near-death pioneer Raymond Moody. In his elaborate vision described in his book *Ordered to Return* in which his guide was no less than Jesus himself, he was shown a variety of hellish experiences, some which were on the earth- plane and others in other realms. In all of these places, there were beings of light standing by the lost souls, and these angels were trying to get them to change their thoughts. Ritchie also relates that Jesus told him that he would draw ALL people to himself, echoing that great Universalist passage, John 12:32.

The prolific liberal Christian writer, Methodist theologian, psychical researcher, and committed Universalist Leslie Weatherhead states in *The Christian Agnostic*, "Hell may last as long as sinful humanity lasts, but that does not mean that any individual will remain in it all that time. The time of purging can only continue until purification is reached. And a God driven to employ endless hell would be a God turned fiend himself, defeated in his original purpose … but God will never desert the soul." It should be noted that Rev. Weatherhead was converted to Universalism in theology school as a result of a powerful mystical experience.

Kevin Williams, webmaster of the "#1" NDE website on Google and Yahoo (www.near-death.com), is a committed Universalist. In his book, *Nothing Better Than Death*, he states that, "Universal salvation is the concept that everyone will eventually attain salvation and go to heaven. This is a foreign concept to most Christians today, although it was not to many early Christians. Many Christians today cannot accept the NDE because it generally affirms Universal Salvation. While it is true Universal Salvation is generally affirmed in NDEs, it is not true that everyone enters heaven immediately upon death. It is well-documented in NDEs people going to hell upon death. However, NDEs show hell to be a temporary spiritual condition, much like Catholic purgatory, not eternal damnation."

Near-death researcher and experiencer Nancy Evans Bush who is a retired pastoral counselor of the Congregational Church has recently completed the analysis of 31 research studies on negative near-death experiences that shows, in addition to the fact that "good" people sometimes have negative experiences, there is evidence that these experiences are for instruction and that eventually, "a positive experience is likely to emerge."

This same view is shared by internist and near-death researcher Barbara Rommer who wrote *Blessing in Disguise* about negative near-death experiences. Rommer reports that negative experiences often change to positive, and it is her belief that if they are allowed to continue, the white light of God and peaceful experiences will and do unfold.

Psychical researcher F. W. H. Myers, in his book *Human Personality and Its Survival of Bodily Death*, notes that in veridical cases indicative of afterlife, there seems to be a, "disintegration of selfishness, malevolence, pride. And is this not a natural result of any cosmic moral evolution? ... the student of these narratives will, I think, discover throughout them uncontradicted indications of the presence of Love, the growth of Joy, and the submission to Law."

A deathbed vision occurs when a person is dying and tells people in the room what he or she is seeing at the point of death. In their book, *At the Hour of Death*, psychical researchers Karlis Osis and Erlendur Haraldsson note that in a cross-cultural study of 1700 people in the United States and India, only one of these cases was hellish. In all cases, the take-away person was an apparition of a dead person, either a dead loved one or a religious figure. This was true, regardless of whether the person was Christian, Hindu, Jew, Moslem, or unbeliever.

Conclusion

While a good many researchers like the Unitarian Sir Alister Hardy, author of *The Spiritual Nature of Man* and founder of the Religious Experience Research Centre (formerly at Oxford) at the University of Wales Lampeter have had religious experiences themselves, there are a few like the Unitarian William James, author of *The Varieties of Religious Experience*, who have not. My own commitment to Universalism is based in part on my own two mystical experiences of God but also on the testimony of hundreds of people I have interviewed and the thousands more I've read about in the works of the authors I have cited. Although this ongoing research has expanded the known "data" available, in a very real way, I don't know any more than I knew fifteen years ago when I wrote this conclusion in my book, *Visions of God from the Near-Death Experience*:

God is love.
We are all connected.
We are all part of God.
God's plan for the Universe may be beyond humanity's understanding,
    but we are a part of it.
Hell is the absence of God.
Hell is the land of the self-preoccupied who have shut out the Love
    of God and others.

It is never too late to call out to God, even from Hell.
It is never too late to turn to the ones who love you and go toward
The Light.

CHAPTER 9

Mystical Religious Experiences and Christian Universalism

~

The very personal, direct experience of God—when the barriers between the human being and God's Universe dissolve— is termed a mystical religious experience. Both the Hebrew Scriptures and the New Testament tell of many who were immersed in the Spirit of God. Within their pages, we are allowed to share the visions of God through the eyes of the Prophet Isaiah (Is 1:1, 6:1-8) and to enter into the ecstatic mystical experience as told by St. Paul (II Cor 12:2). For Christians, Jesus is the one who most perfectly became One with God (Jn 10:30). In addition to those named in the Bible, "saints", "sages", and "mystics" blessed with this intimate knowledge of God have existed from the beginning of time, and we are fortunate to have the writings of many who were emboldened to act in their societies following their experiences. (Later in this chapter, some of the well-known Universalist mystics will be discussed.) But were you aware that religious mystics are still among us today? Over the past hundred years, researchers in the scientific study of religion have been able to determine that "mystical" experiences of God are not really so rare! (Data from this scientific inquiry will be explored later in this chapter.) When I have taught adult Sunday school classes or Psychology of Religion classes on the topic of mystical religious experience, inevitably those who can recall their own mystical experience of God understand me perfectly while those who have not had this kind of personal experience often remain skeptical! In this chapter, I hope to offer some personal and social science evidence which will help to expand the understanding of this phenomenon.

To me, the fact that everyone has not had a personal mystical experience is a source of sadness. The great dream of all mystics is that we could, in the words of William Blake, "cleanse the doors of perception" so that all might experience directly the loving presence of God in the here-and-now. In reality, "unknown" and "anonymous" mystics have been discovered among ordinary people in almost half the population. Two more facts regarding mystical experiences help to put this experience into perspective: The first is that mystical religious experiences usually occur only once or twice in the lifetimes of about half of those reporting them, and the second is that mystical religious experiences, although always profound, definitely vary in intensity from one person to another. Some years ago I was watching a television interview of Mother Theresa who related that she had only *one* mystical experience—a vision of Jesus telling her to go to India and serve the poor! When I teach, I often make the analogy that some of us received a *candle* of light while Jesus received a *beacon*!

Mystical religious experiences are categorized as either "spontaneous" (they "just happen!") or "sought-after." Meditation is the *only* safe way to induce this experience, but there is no guarantee that meditation will produce the desired outcome. All true mystical experiences serve to reinforce what Jesus taught about God's love for us. Mystics through the ages have reminded us to stay the true course, reject dogma, and not let mechanical ritual substitute for good works and kindness. Like Jesus, Christian mystics have often been at odds with the church leaders when those leaders have put authority, church business, and theological interpretation above the compassion of God.

Jesus promised the continuous presence of the Holy Spirit (Jn 14:26), and St. Paul expressed his unquestioned belief that the direct experience of God is open to everyone (II Cor 3:18). Conservative Christian scholar Luke Timothy Johnson correctly notes that mystical religious experiences described in the New Testament are often ignored in modern studies of Christian origins. This direct contact between God and humanity in the New Testament is also discussed by moderate Christian scholar James D. G. Dunn, in his book *Jesus and the Spirit*.

Universalism Among Mystics

Universalist theology is rooted in religious mystical experience and can be found in mystics writing as early as the second century and continuing throughout the Dark Ages, the Reformation, and the Age of Enlightenment. Mystic and researcher Evelyn Underhill considers these prominent Universalist mystics to be among the greatest: Clement of Alexandria (160-220), Origen (183-253), Macarius of Egypt (295-386), Gregory of Nyssa (335-394), John Scotus Erigena (810-877), Jacob Boehme (1575-1624), and Jane Lead(e) (1625-1704). The Carmelite Priest and mystical researcher Bruno Borchert adds these Universalists: Gregory of Nazianze (329-390) and Hans Denck (1500-1527). In my view, no list of Universalist mystics would be complete without George De Benneville (1703-1793).

Jane Lead, who founded a society of Universalists called the Philadelphians in seventeenth century London, described her mystical experience in which the nature of post-mortem punishment was revealed to her. Recorded in her book, *The Enochian Walks with God*, she states that God's love triumphs, that punishment is for reforming, and that all are reconciled with God in the end. George De Benneville— physician, preacher, and mystic —wrote of his Universalist mystical religious experience and his in-depth near-death experience in his book entitled, *The Life and Trance of Dr. George De Benneville*. Like Jane Lead, these personal experiences convinced De Benneville that Hell is for purification and that, in the end, *all* will be united with God.

Throughout the history of Christianity, mystics not identified formally as Universalists have nevertheless advocated Universalist ideas. This is hardly surprising, as in the West the Catholic Church had condemned Origen's form of Universalism as heretical, and Universalism had to go underground until the Reformation. In contrast, the Eastern Church (Oriental Orthodox, a.k.a. Nestorian Church or Assyrian Church of the East) accepted Universalist theology. Greats such as Theodore of Mopsuestia placed Universalism solidly in the liturgy. Additionally, Universalism is recorded in the Eastern Church's thirteenth century *Book of the Bee* (Chapter LX). Universalist thinking continues in less emphatic form in the liturgy of the Eastern Church today.

A good example of Universalism in the writings of "unofficial" Universalist mystics is the great fourteenth century English mystic, Julian of Norwich. Though her Universalist mystical experiences of God were contrary to Catholic Church teachings of Hell and Purgatory, she wrote that both must be true in some sense, though she did not see it. This "dance" she did between church dogma and her mystical religious experiences was enough to keep her in the good graces of church officials. Nevertheless, her Universalism shines through. She writes: "All shall be well, and all shall be well, and all manner of thing shall be well ... And He is very Father and very Mother of Nature: and all natures that He hath made to flow out of Him to work His will shall be restored and brought again into Him by the salvation of man through the working of Grace...All this being so, it seemed to me that it was impossible that every kind of thing should be well, as our Lord revealed at this time ... And to this I had no other answer as a revelation from our Lord except this: "What is impossible to you is not impossible to me. I shall preserve my word in everything and I shall make everything well." Thus she echoes the Universalist message of St. Paul that God will be "all in all" (I Cor 15:28). It is this Universality of God's love for *all* and God's presence in *all* that is the hallmark of all mystical religious experience whether or not theological statements of Universalism are proclaimed. As George Fox, founder of the Quaker movement, was known to repeat: "All creatures in God, and God in all creatures."

Mystical religious experiences are not limited to Christianity and are Universal, as expressed by the early twentieth century mystic and researcher Evelyn Underhill (Anglican): "This unmistakable experience has been achieved by the mystics of every religion; and when we read their statements, we know that all are speaking of the same thing." William James, the first American-born psychologist, believed that, "The founders of every church owed their power originally to the fact of their direct personal communication with the divine." If God loves us all, how could this be otherwise? This case for Universality has been well documented by other Christian writers, including John Hick (Universalist) who bases his Universalism in part on his own mystical experiences of God and Bruno Borchert (Carmelite priest).

Early Research

In studying the accounts of mystics from Biblical times to the present, it is easy to hear the recurring themes of 1) The continuity of God's love, and 2) The Oneness with God and the Universe. However, some of the first modern philosophers and theorists, lacking any objective data to support their views, dismissed religion as superstition and labeled mystics as having mental problems. The best example of this faulty reasoning is Sigmund Freud who pronounced that religious founders like Jesus were psychotic and that religious people were neurotic. Fortunately, at the time Freud was making unsupported claims (that would later be refuted), a champion arose to counter his flawed theories.

Over a hundred years ago, William James, the first American psychologist, began his serious study of religious experience. His classic work, *The Varieties of Religious Experience*, was published in 1901 but is still in print today. Using the basic tools of observation and case studies, he began to research religious visions and mystical experience. James was able to formulate some working hypotheses on the nature of religious experiences, and much of what he hypothesized has subsequently been tested in large-scale research projects that have subsequently validated his observations.

Modern Research

The big news today in the study of mystical religious experiences is sheer numbers! Social scientists now have documented thousands of people who have come forward to tell of their direct experience of God. Researchers can now state with absolute certainty that Freud was wrong—the number of people with personal experience of God is at least eight times greater than the number of people who have suffered psychotic episodes!

Large-scale surveys on mystical experience began in 1969 when Alister Hardy founded the Religious Experience Research Unit at Oxford University. In order to research mystical religious experience within the general population, Sir Hardy made an appeal to the general public via newspapers and pamphlets which asked the question, "Have you ever been aware of or influenced by a presence or power, whether you call it 'God' or not, which is different from your everyday self?" Readers were invited to send him their responses. Ten years later, Hardy published a book based on the first 3,000 responses he had received to this question. The Alister Hardy Religious Experience Research Center at Oxford also found that 95% of reported mystical experiences in their British national sample were positive.

The next significant step taken by social scientists to objectify research on this topic was in 1977 by David Hay and Ann Morisy. Using the same question about the experience of God used in the previous study, they studied a random sample of 1,865 British persons (rather than a self-selected group as in the first survey), and 35% responded "yes" to the question. Repeating the Alister Hardy question on mystical religious experience ten years later, a British Gallup Poll found that the number responding "yes" had risen to 48%. In Australia, a similar study the same year found 44% of the population reporting "yes" to the same question.

Between the appeal in the British newspaper for accounts and the objective large-scale population survey, Andrew Greely and his colleagues at the National Opinion Research Center at the University of Chicago began their surveying using a similar question: *"Have you ever felt as though you were very close to a powerful spiritual force that seemed to lift you out of yourself?"* A national sample of 1,467 Americans showed 39% responding "yes." Over the years, repeated national samples have shown that the number of people responding affirmatively to this question has varied from 35% to 50%. In a poll of Poles, Andrezej Kokoszka of the Copernicus School of Medicine in Krakow found that 54% of those surveyed reported at least one profoundly altered state of consciousness. These included 1) "Experience contact with a Divine Being or God" (36%) 2) "Experience of the impression that you understood everything, only it was impossible to utter this impression" (often called "cosmic consciousness") (28%), and 3) "Experience of the feeling of being One with the Universe" (16%).

Some evidence supports an increase in mystical experiences. Three in-depth British studies in which the respondents were interviewed rather than surveyed yielded positive response rates of over 60%. One-fourth of the respondents reported that they had never told anyone else of this experience for fear of being thought "mentally ill" or "stupid." When Americans were recently surveyed with the question: *"In general, how often would you say you had experienced God's presence or a spiritual force that felt very close to you?,"* an incredible 86% reported that this had happened to them one or more times!

Mystics Are Happier!

A survey of British by Hay and Morisy noted that people reporting mystical religious experiences tended to have greater psychological well-being than those who report no mystical religious experiences. In his survey of Americans, Andrew Greely noted the same phenomenon:

"Mystics are happier." Ralph Hood has demonstrated a correlation between high scores on a scale of mystical experience and measures of mental health. Prof. Hay notes that studies on mysticism and mental health refute Sigmund Freud's hypothesis that religion was symptomatic of neurosis and religious experience was perhaps temporary psychosis. Hay further notes that studies in England, the United States, and Australia consistently show that mysticism is more apt to be reported by people in the upper-middle and professional middle classes rather than the lower classes. This disproves the Marxist hypothesis that religion is the "opiate of the masses." Also, the hypothesis of the sociologist Dirkheim that religious experience is typically an "effervescent group phenomenon," is refuted by a Gallup Poll survey in Britain in 1987 which found that 60% of accounts of religious experience occurred in the context of solitude.

Research into the mental health of those who have mystical experiences has shown mystical experiencers to be normal or healthy. My own feeling is that this may be due to the fact that it takes a certain amount of guts to come forward and tell others that you have been personally touched by God. This has become easier over the past forty years because research in the social sciences has documented that mystical experiences are common. Still, the tendency is for people not to come forward with mystical experiences unless they are sure that the people listening will accept them.

Differentiating from the Occult

People who engage in occult practices like to pretend their practices are mystic, but there is an easy test to determine the difference. The occult has to do with manipulating the paranormal for selfish personal ends such as influencing a person to become your lover, inflicting ill upon a person (as in the case of Voodoo dolls), or seeing the future with the intent of changing an outcome in your own favor. The most famous example of occult practices is found in the first book of Samuel (I Sam 28:3-16) in which King Saul asks the medium of Endor to perform necromancy and conger up the spirit of the dead prophet Samuel in order to foresee the outcome of the next day's battle. In short, the occult is all about, "me, me, me!" Mysticism is about God and from God. Nothing evil ever comes from God (Jas 1:12-17). Whereas mystical experiences are positive and lead to happiness, psychologist Michael Argyle notes occult experiences have the opposite effect.

Research on Children

Interestingly, children's acknowledgment of the presence of God declines with age. When Finnish researcher Kalevi Tamminen asked children ages 7 to 20, "Have you at times felt that God was particularly close to you?, 84% of the first-graders acknowledged the presence of God. Interestingly, by the end of high school, the number had declined to 47%. The modern world is often hostile to spirituality. There is also evidence that people may have mystical experiences but deny them. Carl Sagan, the famous physicist, once stated that he had felt on several occasions that his dead parents had tried to contact him, but he dismissed this as being impossible. He is unusual, as most people alter their beliefs when confronted with their own personal experience. On this topic, almost 40% of Americans report contact with the dead, according to the National Opinion Research Center.

Case Studies

Despite the incredible variety of human beings and human cultures, all true mystical religious experiences have an underlying similarity. Most importantly, mystics never "let go" of their experience, and it permanently alters their perspective on life. For those who know this experience personally, as well as for those who are gaining these insights vicariously, I wanted to present some of the powerfully moving accounts of mystical religious experiences expressed in the words of the mystics themselves. These cases give a greater insight into the experience itself as well as its effect on the individual.

I will begin with two of my own mystical religious experiences which were spontaneous. The first was one that is quite commonly reported. In fact, in a sermon some years ago, Rev. Horace Westwood described his own mystical experience that was virtually identical to this one of mine:

It occurred in the winter of 1973 when I was 29 and a doctoral student in psychology at the University of Northern Colorado. "Late one cold afternoon, I was in the parking lot with my back to the panorama of the Rocky Mountains, looking instead at a small dead tree in a snow bank. All at once, I was lifted up, and I was one with God and the Universe. I felt timeless and immortal. A few moments later, I was back to my normal state, but the moment has never left me. It left me knowing that we are all a part of God and that God is with us always."

Mystical experiences can happen at *any* time. St. Teresa had a mystical experience while cooking eggs for her convent—she reportedly burned the eggs! My second mystical experience occurred during my mid-forties while teaching at the University of Houston: I was at a football game in the Astrodome, waiting in the concession line: "All at once, I felt as if I were inside the minds of all the people around me and that I could feel what they were feeling. I could feel their happiness, their love for their friends and family, and their joy at being together. Though it only lasted for a few moments, it was like tapping into the Spirit of God. I had often wondered what God gets out of Creation, and I got an answer that day: God gets to be all of us!"

Mystical experiences vary widely from mild to overwhelming. Mine were definitely not of the magnitude of St. Paul or even Ralph Waldo Emerson, but I present them as examples of mild mystical experiences.

The following account is from a 56-year-old British female, one of the modern cases from Alister Hardy's Religious Experience Research Unit at Oxford University that appeared in his book, *The Spiritual Nature of Man*: "On this occasion I found instead that I was overtaken by an intense feeling of affection for and unity with everyone around as they ran to catch buses, took children shopping, or joyfully met their friends. The feeling was so strong that I wanted to leave my silent vigil and join them in their urgent living. This sense of 'Oneness' is basic to what I understand of religion. Hitherto I think I had only experienced it so irresistibly towards a few individuals—sometimes toward my children or when in love. The effect of the experience has been, I think, a permanent increase in my awareness that we are 'members one of another,' a consequent greater openness toward all and a widening of my concern for others."

The next account appeared in the 1937 edition of the Universalist magazine, *The Christian Leader* and is from author Mary Austin who had a mystical experience as a child: "I must have been between five and six, when this experience happened to me. It was a summer morning, and the child I was had walked down through the orchard alone and come out on the brow of a sloping hill where there was grass and the wind blowing and one tall tree reaching into the infinite immensities of blueness. Quite suddenly, after a moment of quietness there, earth and sky and tree and windblown grass and the child in the midst of them came alive together with a pulsing light of consciousness. There was a wild foxglove at the child's feet and a bee dozing about. And to this day, I recall the swift inclusive awareness of each for the whole

— I in them, and they in me, and all of us enclosed in a warm, lucent bubble of livingness. I remember the child looking everywhere for the source of this happy wonder, and at last she questioned — 'God'— because it was the only awesome word she knew. Deep inside like the murmurous swinging of a bell she heard the answer, 'God, God.' How long this ineffable moment lasted I never knew. It broke like a bubble at the sudden singing of a bird, and the wind blew and the world was the same as ever, only never quite the same."

Obviously, how people interpret their experience depends on their time and culture. Regarding my own mystical experiences, I freely admit that these experiences reinforced my belief that God communicates with human beings. I also interpret them in the same way as the great contemporary Universalist theologian, John Hick, who notes that he too has had mystical experiences that convinced him, "we know the Transcendent Holy Presence to be profoundly good to exist and in which the unknown future holds no possible threat."

The following are two mystical religious experiences of John Hick, the world's foremost Universalist / pluralist philosopher, extracted from his autobiography. His first mystical experience (which was spontaneous) occurred at age 18 years while riding on the top deck of a bus: "As everyone will be very conscious who can themselves remember such a moment, all descriptions are inadequate. But it was as though the skies opened up and light poured down and filled me with a sense of overflowing joy, in response to an immense transcendent goodness and love. I remember that I couldn't help smiling broadly — smiling back, as it were, at God — though if any of the other passengers were looking, they must have thought that I was a lunatic, grinning at nothing."

His next mystical experience was the "sought-after" variety and occurred many years later when Dr. Hick was practicing Buddhist meditation: "I have once, but so far only once, experienced what was to me a startling breakthrough into a new form or level of consciousness. I was in that second stage and when eventually I opened my eyes the world was quite different in two ways. Whereas normally I am here, and the environment is there, separate from me, there was now no such distinction; and more importantly, the total universe of which I was part was friendly, benign, good, so that there could not possibly be anything to fear or worry about. It was a state of profound delight in being. This only lasted a short time, probably not more than two minutes."

The great twentieth-century mystical researcher, Evelyn Underhill, was herself a mystic. Early in her career, she described herself as a "passionate amateur of experience" and was very much interested in comparative religion. Later in her career, because of her mystical experiences, she identified herself primarily as a Christian, although she continued to be interested in world religion. The following mystical experience occurred to her in 1923 at the age of 48 years and is at the time of her centering on Christianity. This account is from Armstrong's biography of her: "Such lights as one gets are now different in type: *all* overwhelming in their emotional result: quite independent 'sensible devotion', more quiet, calm, expansive, like intellectual intuitions yet not quite that either. Thus yesterday I saw and felt *how* it actually is, that we are in Christ and he is in us—the interpretation of the Spirit— and all of us merged together in him actually, and so fitly described as his body. The way to full intercessory power must, I think, be along this path."

The following is an account of a middle-aged female from Richard Bucke's *Cosmic Consciousness*:

"I was losing my consciousness, my identity, I was powerless to hold myself. Now came a period of rapture so intense that the Universe stood still, as if amazed at the unutterable majesty of the spectacle! Only one in all the infinite Universe! The All-loving, the Perfect One! The Perfect Wisdom, truth, love, and purity! And with the rapture came the insight. In that same wonderful moment of what might be called supernatural bliss, came illumination... What joy when I saw there was no break in the chain—not a link left out—everything in its time and place. Worlds, systems, all bended in one harmonious whole. Universal light, synonymous with Universal love!"

In this account from *Cosmic Consciousness*, a 35-year old journalist, Paul Tyner, describes "the crowning experience of my life:" "Now, indeed, it is plain, that being lifted up he shall lift all men with him-has lifted, is lifting and must ever continue to lift out of the very essence of his transcendent humanity. Immortality is no longer an hypothesis of the theologian, a figment of the imagination, a dream of the poet. Men shall live forever, because man, invincible to all effects of time and change, and even of murderous violence, lives today in the fullness of life and power that he enjoyed in his thirty-third year, with only added glory of goodness and greatness and beauty...This is the truth given age upon age to all men in all lands, and persistently misunderstood—the truth at last to be seen of all men in its fullness and purity."

Hannah Whitall Smith was a writer and the wife of a Quaker minister. In Chapter 22 of her book, *The Unselfishness of God and*

How I Discovered It, she relates two mystical religious experiences of Universalism. Interestingly, some "Christian" publishers delete this chapter on Universalism. She writes:

"And with this a veil seemed to be withdrawn from before the plans of the universe, and I saw that it was true, as the Bible says, that 'as in Adam all die, even so in Christ should all be made alive.' As was the first, even so was the second. The 'all' in one case could not in fairness mean less than the 'all' in the other. I saw therefore that the remedy must necessarily be equal to the disease, the salvation must be as universal as the fall ... God is the Creator of every human being, therefore He is the Father of each one, and they are all His children; and Christ died for everyone, and is declared to be 'the propitiation not for our sins only, but also for the sins of the whole world' (1 John 2:2). However great the ignorance therefore, or however grievous the sin, the promise of salvation is positive and without limitations ... The how and the when I could not see; but the one essential fact was all I needed—somewhere and somehow God was going to make everything right for all the creatures He had created. My heart was at rest about it forever."

This next account of a Universalist mystical experience is from Sir Hardy's *The Spiritual Nature of Man*, and describes Rev. Dr. Leslie Weatherhead's youthful experience: "This is the only way I know in which to describe the moment, for there was nothing to see at all. I felt caught up into some tremendous sense of being within a loving, triumphant and shining purpose. I never felt more humble. I never felt more exalted. A most curious, but overwhelming sense possessed me and filled me with ecstasy. I felt that all was well for mankind-how poor the words seem! The word 'well' is so poverty stricken. All men were shining and glorious beings who in the end would enter incredible joy. Beauty, music, joy, love immeasurable and a glory unspeakable they would inherit. Of this they were heirs."

In this account from Prof. David Hay's *Exploring Inner Space*, a female writer recalls a mystical religious experience from childhood— an account that echoes an experience of the famous mystic Julian of Norwich: "My father used to take all the family for a walk on Sunday evenings. On one such walk, we wandered across a narrow path through a field of high, ripe corn. I lagged behind, and found myself alone. Suddenly, heaven blazed upon me. I was enveloped in golden light, I was conscious of a presence, so kind, so loving, so bright, so consoling, so commanding, existing apart from me but so close. I heard no sound. But words fell into my mind quite clearly—everything is all right. Everybody will be all right."

The following account is that of Dr. Richard Bucke, a Canadian neuropsychiatrist and scholar of comparative religion whose mystical religious experience inspired him to research and write *Cosmic Consciousness*: "All at once, without warning of any kind, I found myself wrapped in a flame-colored cloud. For an instant I thought of fire, an immense conflagration somewhere close by in that great city; the next, I knew that the fire was within myself. Directly afterward there came upon me a sense of exultation, of immense joyousness accompanied or immediately followed by an intellectual illumination impossible to describe. Among other things, I did not merely come to believe, but I saw that the universe is not composed of dead matter, but is, on the contrary, a living Presence; I became conscious in myself of eternal life. It was not a conviction that I would have eternal life, but a consciousness that I possessed eternal life then; I saw that all men are immortal; that the cosmic order is such that without any peradventure all things work together for the good of each and all; that the foundation principle of the world, of all the worlds, is what we call love, and that the happiness of each and all is in the long run absolutely certain. The vision lasted a few seconds and was gone; but the memory of it and the sense of the reality of what it taught has remained during the quarter of a century which has since elapsed. I knew that what the vision showed was true. I had attained to a point of view from which I saw that it must be true. That view, that conviction, I may say that consciousness, has never, even during periods of the deepest depression, been lost."

The following is an account of a 55-year-old male taken from Prof. Timothy Beardsworth's *A Sense of Presence*: "One lunch time I had been helping to dry dishes after the meal, and was standing before the open drawer of the sideboard putting knives and forks away. I was not thinking of anything, apart from vague attention to the job I was doing. Suddenly, without warning, I was flooded with the most intense blue-white light I have ever seen. Words can never adequately nor remotely touch the depth of this experience. It was like looking into the face of the sun, magnified several times in its light-intensity. It would be truer to say that I lost all sense of self in total immersion in Light. But more 'real' than the Light itself was the unbearable ecstasy that accompanied it. All sense of time or self disappeared, yet it could only have been a fraction of a second. I knew only a sense of infinite dimension, and a knowledge that this was the Spirit of God Almighty, which was the hidden Life-Light-Love in all men, all life and all creation. I knew that nothing existed apart from this Spirit. It was infinite Love, Peace, Law, Power, Creation and the Ultimate Truth and Perfection. It was all Wisdom, Tolerance, Understanding and Eternal Life for all people. I also knew that had I been suffering from any so-called incurable disease whatsoever, I would have become instantly whole. Then after the fraction of a second—I became myself again, still standing beside the open drawer putting knives and forks away. That one moment was and remains the most vital moment of my life, for there has never been a repetition. But out of it was born the Mission to which I have for many years dedicated my life ..."

Summary

Regarding mystical religious experiences, it is valid to say that,

1. They happen to a large percentage of the population.
2. The overwhelming majority of those people are normal, healthy, and no more apt to be mentally ill than the general population.
3. They change people's lives.

Modern accounts assure us that truly God is with us always, and that in time, "All flesh shall see the salvation of God" (Lk 3:6). Until then, the Bible can be our source for accessing the Holy Spirit promised to us by Jesus, and Jesus' teachings instruct us in the way to build the Kingdom of God within our midst. Testimony of those in the Bible and that of the mystics assure us all that God is there for *all* of us, and mystical religious experiences serve as a continuing reminder of the loving presence of God in our lives.

The Spirit of God has been and is with us always. There is no doubt we live in God.

CHAPTER 10

The Near-Death Experience and Christian Universalism

O f all the theological explanations for the near-death experience (NDE), the Doctrine of Universal Salvation, also known as Universalism, is the most compatible with contemporary NDE accounts.

Universalism embraces the idea that God is too good to condemn humankind to Eternal Hell and that, sooner or later, all humanity will be saved. Interestingly, a belief in Universal Salvation can be found in virtually all the world's major religions (Vincent, 2000, pp. 6-8). It is particularly essential to Zoroastrianism, the religion of the Magi (Vincent, 1999, pp. 9-10 and 46-47).

The Universalist theology that acknowledges a temporary Hellish state for those who need some "shaping up" before proceeding to their ultimate reward is termed more specifically "Restorative Universalism." In my book *Visions of God from the Near-Death Experience*, I included a chapter on frightening NDEs, coupled with Hell as portrayed in sacred scriptures. My intention then was to present the topic of Universal Salvation in the world's religions from a spiritual perspective (Vincent, 1994). In this article, I want to show that Christian Universalism, a doctrine with solid support in the New Testament, blends seamlessly with the experience of NDErs.

By exploring the connections between the NDE and Universalist theology, I have no interest in reviving the so-called "Religious Wars" in the NDE movement (Ellwood, 2000; Ring, 2000; Sabom, 2000a, 2000b). I do hope to offer a source of comfort to NDErs, both Christian and non-Christian, who may have had their experience marginalized by assaults from Fundamentalist or Conservative Christians. They can be assured that a more loving alternative to Christian "exclusivity" (that is, "only Christians go to Heaven") exists within the same New Testament they have known since childhood.

In a recent national poll for *Religion & Ethics Newsweekly* and *U. S. News & World Report* (Mitofsky International and Edison Media Research, 2002), only 19 percent of Christians and 7 percent of non-Christians stated a belief that their religion was the only true religion. This contrasted with a 1965 poll in which 65 percent of Protestants and 51 percent of Catholics reported that "belief in Jesus Christ as Savior was absolutely necessary for Salvation" (Glock and Stark, 1965).

Americans appear to be becoming more Universalist in their orientation. The 2002 study also found that "an individual's spiritual experience (as opposed to doctrines and beliefs) is the most important part of religion" was answered in the affirmative by 69 percent of Christians and 73 percent of non-Christians (Mitofsky International and Edison Media Research, 2002). Americans also appear to be more spiritually aware, or at least more willing to admit it. In 2002, 86 percent of Americans stated that they had "experienced God's presence or a spiritual force that felt very close to you one or more times" (Mitofsky International and Edison Media Research, 2002). Spirituality has always been part of religious experience. In this article, I will explore how Universalist ideas are expressed in the Bible, and, more importantly, how Universalism helps place the near death experience within the context of Christian theology.

Validity of the Bible

To examine these questions, we must first consider the status of the Bible and theological interpretations of it. In polls regarding the validity of the Bible, about one-third of Americans reported a belief that the Bible is "the actual Word of God" (about as many as report being Fundamentalist). One-sixth (about the number of non-Christians in America) described it as a "book of fables, legends, history, and moral precepts." One-half believed it to be the "inspired Word of God but that not everything should be taken literally" (Mitofsky International and Edison Media Research, 2002, p.2; Wood, 1989, pp. 130 and 361). These views of the general population reflect modern scholarship regarding the Bible. Today, Biblical inerrancy is a view adhered to by only the most Fundamentalist scholars (Borg, 2001).

The Bible contains a treasure trove of ancient accounts of mystical religious experiences. Conservative Christian scholar Luke Timothy Johnson (1998) correctly noted that modern studies of Christian origins ignore the mystical religious experiences so clearly described in the New Testament. Moderate Christian scholar James D. G. Dunn noted, in referring to Jesus, that "there is no incidence of a healing miracle that falls clearly outside the general character of psycho-somatic illness" (1975/1997, p. 71). Nevertheless, his book is a study on what may be called "communicative theism," the direct contact between God and humanity in the New Testament. Even the liberal Jesus Seminar voiced no doubt that Jesus appeared to some of his followers after his death (Funk and The Jesus Seminar, 1998).

From the time the Bible was written to the present, individuals have reported mystical experiences (Argyle, 2000; Hick, 1999; James, 1901/1958). The NDE is unique among the categories of mystical union with God (Borg, 1997) because of its identifiable "trigger." The big question is: How much credibility should one give to reports of mystical experiences in the Bible, as most are not first-person accounts but rather written down as "much-told tales" following many years of oral tradition? As stated above, most scholars do not consider the Bible to be inerrant. In light of this, it becomes untenable in theological interpretation to base one's theological program on one or two Bible verses. For example, the basis of papal authority is inferred from two verses in the Gospel of Matthew (Matthew 16:18-19). Even more difficult is justification for the Trinity, which is not in the Bible and can at best only be inferred by the fact that God, God's Spirit, and Jesus are mentioned together in two verses (Matthew 28:19; 2 Corinthians 13:14). I will discuss further below how theology can be based on a preponderance of verses in the New Testament.

Christian Universalism

At this time, let me state that I am a Unitarian Universalist Christian and, like most Liberal Christians, I believe that God was in Jesus, but not that Jesus was God. Universalism as a theological system traces its history back to Origen (185-254 CE). The Universalist Church in North America was, for a time during the nineteenth century, the fifth or sixth largest denomination in the United States (Howe, 1993). The Universalist Church merged with the Unitarians in 1961, and Unitarian Universalist Christians still make up a majority of our members worldwide. In the United States, ours has developed into an interfaith church in which Unitarian Universalist Christians comprise only a minority.

As stated above, there are several variants of Christian Universalism. Some Universalists believe that God will save you "no matter what." This is a variant of "Jesus Saves" theology, except that "Jesus Saves Everybody" by his atoning sacrifice (Howe, 1993, pp. 34-35). Another variant is the belief that Christians will be saved immediately, and all others will be saved after becoming believers (Howe, 1993). Restorative Universalism assumes a judgment ("life review" in NDE terminology) and punishment for some, followed by Universal Salvation for all.

Today, most Christians who profess a belief in Universal Salvation belong to variety of other denominations. Despite their questions about doctrine, most Liberal Christians choose to remain within more mainline denominations, most often for reasons of tradition. Examples of prominent contemporary Universalist Christian theologians in other denominations are Jan Bonda of the Dutch Reformed Church (1993/1998); Tom Harpur, an Anglican (1986); John Hick of the United Reformed Church (Hick, Pinnock, McGarth, Geivett, and Phillips, 1995), and Thomas Talbott, an Independent Christian (Talbott, 1999). It is noteworthy that, in addition to being a Christian scholar, Tom Harpur was a near-death researcher, and he included a strong Universalist Christian statement at the end of his book, *Life after Death* (1991).

Christian theologies are systems created to explain the diverse and conflicting accounts given by the various authors of the New Testament. Often theologians will arrive at differing interpretations of what the words in a particular Bible verse mean. For example, "I am the way, and the truth, and the life. No one comes to the Father except through me" (John 14:6) is a primary verse used by "Jesus Saves" theologians; however, this verse has been interpreted by Liberal Christians as meaning that salvation comes from following the teachings of Jesus, rather than through his death on the cross (Borg, 2001; Harpur, 1986; Hick, 1993a).

In an article in *Christianity Today* entitled, "The Gift of Salvation," Timothy George (1997) made the case for "Jesus Saves" theology by citing just 23 verses from the New Testament. By my own calculations, there were 139 verses in the New Testament supporting "Jesus Saves" theology; 551 verses supporting Salvation by Good Works, with 389 of those verses being the words of Jesus himself; and 178 verses supporting Universal Salvation, including 31 verses that speak to Hell not being permanent. It is worth noting that a fourth theological position, the Doctrine of Predestination, has 77 verses to support it (Hastings, Grant, and Rowley, 1953). One can see from the sheer magnitude of data that Salvation by Good Works has the most support, followed by Universal Salvation for All. The two taken together form the case for Christian Restorative Universalism.

Universalism and the NDE

When it comes to the near-death experience, Universalism appears to be the most compatible theological position. Why is that so? Let us explore some basics of Christian Restorative Universalism and the NDE. NDEs often begin with an "out-of-body" experience (OBE). The Bible records this 2000-year-old OBE by St. Paul: I know a person in Christ who fourteen years ago was caught up to the third Heaven-whether in the body or out of the body I do not know; God knows. And I know that such a person-whether in the body or out of the body I do not know; God knows-was caught up into Paradise and heard things that were not to be told, that no mortal is permitted to repeat. (2 Corinthians 12:2-5).

One of the most commonly reported characteristics of a deep NDE is the experience of Light or Being of Light (Vincent, 1994). Some NDErs feel that this Light represents God or God's emissary, as in the following: "I was in the Universe and I was Light. It takes all the fear of dying out of you. It was Heavenly. I was in the Presence of God." (Vincent, 1994, p. 27)

"I went directly into the Light, and my pain ceased. There was a feeling of extreme peace." (Vincent, 1994, p. 27)

In the Bible we read: God is light, and in him there is no darkness at all. (1 John 1:5) Every generous act of giving, with every perfect gift, is from above, coming down from the Father of lights. (James 1:17) He who is the blessed and only Sovereign, the King of kings and Lord of lords. It is he alone who has immortality and dwells in unapproachable light. (1 Timothy 6:15-16)

NDErs routinely report an immense amount of unconditional love radiating from the Being of Light:

> "An absolute white Light that is God-all loving. The unification of us with our Creator." (Vincent, 1994, p. 27)

> "I left my body, and I was surrounded by God. It didn't feel male or female, young or old, just me. I was surrounded by Love. ... I looked down at the little girl in bed. ... Later when I realized it was me, I was back in my body." (Vincent, 1994, p. 21)

In the Bible we read: Beloved, let us love one another, because love is from God; everyone who loves is born of God and knows God. Whoever does not love does not know God, for God is love. (1 John 4:7-8) The steadfast love of the Lord never ceases, his mercies never come to an end. (Lamentations 3:22)

NDErs report a feeling of "Oneness with God" and a sensation of being "In God":

> "And deep within me came an instant and wondrous recognition: I, even I, was facing God." (Vincent, 1994, p. 23)

> "It is something which becomes you and you become it. I could say, I was peace; I was love. It was the brightness ... It was part of me." Vincent, 1994, p. 29)

In the Bible we read: For in him we live and move and have our being. (Acts 17:28) For from him and through him and to him are all things. (Romans 11:36) One God and Father of all, who is above all and through all and in all. (Ephesians 4:6)

Sometimes NDErs encounter Jesus in the Light:

"The light was in me and between the molecules, the cells in my body. He was in me—I was in him. ... I knew all things. I saw all things. I was all things. But not me; Jesus had this. As long as I was 'in Him,' and he was 'in me,' I had this power, this glory (for lack of a better word)." (Vincent, 1994, p. 57)

"I left but stood there wanting to help this poor soul (which was in effect me). Then I was on the third level and a voice said, 'choose.' I saw Jesus, the Blessed Mother, and the archangel Michael. My message was unconditional love; learn to love your family; you love others, but learn to love your family." (Vincent, 1994, p. 59)

These accounts recall the Apostle Paul's experience of Jesus. Many scholars consider his account in 1 Corinthians 15:5-8 as the only first-hand account of the resurrection of Jesus (Funk and the Jesus Seminar, 1998; Harpur, 1986; Hick, 1993b). Paul also provided verified secondhand accounts of Jesus' appearance to Peter and James. Researcher Philip Wiebe (1997) maintained that there is no difference between modern-day visions of Jesus and similar visions of Jesus described in the Bible. Although Wiebe excluded NDEs from his research, numerous NDE accounts over the past quarter century attest to face-to-face meetings with Jesus. Curiously, even people of religions other than Christianity have described encounters with Jesus (Rommer, 2000).

Before turning our attention from the Light, it is worth noting that Fundamentalists often counter this common NDE phenomenon with a verse from St. Paul: "Even Satan disguises himself as a being of Light" (2 Corinthians 11:14). This is of dubious relevance for NDEs for two reasons: first, it places too much weight on a single Bible verse; and second, the overwhelming amount of data leaves no doubt that the Light experienced by the NDEr radiates love. Jesus told us how to distinguish false prophets: "You will know them by their fruits" (Matthew 7:16).

When Jesus himself was accused of being Satanic, he explained: And the scribes who came down from Jerusalem said, "He has Beelzebub and by the ruler of the demons he casts out demons." And he called to them and spoke to them in parables, "How can Satan cast out Satan? If a kingdom is divided against itself, that kingdom cannot stand. And if a house is divided against itself, that house will not be able to stand.

And if Satan has risen up against himself and is divided, he cannot stand, but his end is come." (Mark 3:22-26) Fundamentalist Christians cannot have it both ways. The Light cannot represent goodness for a Christian and deception for non-Christians. Satan may be a neon sign, but God is the Light of the Universe.

Jesus told us that God is our Father too: I am ascending to my Father and your Father, to my God and your God. (John 20:17) You have one Father-the one in heaven. (Matthew 23:9) "I will be your Father and you shall be my Sons and Daughters" says the Lord Almighty. (2 Corinthians 6:18) Is there anyone among you who, if your child asks for bread, would give him a stone? Or if the child asks for a fish, would give a snake? If you then who are evil, know how to give good gifts to your children, how much more will your Father in Heaven give good things to those who ask Him? (Matthew 7:9-10) What kind of parent abandons his or her child? Surely not the loving God Jesus talked about.

Judgment or Life Review

Judgment, in NDE terminology, is called "life review." This is usually a positive experience:

"I found myself in a corridor. The corridor did not end. I was not afraid. There was a white light. Very clear white colors of light. Off to the side, I could see shades of gray. Off to the side, I could see my childhood passing, going left to right. I thought to myself, 'I am getting younger.' I did not see my adult life. I felt like I was not alone, but I did not see anybody." (Vincent, 1994, p. 95)

"During the Judgment [it was] like on a Rolodex. I could feel the person by me. I was waiting for the bad to come up, but nothing bad was coming up." (Vincent, 1994, p. 93)

For others, there is a perception of one's effect on other people:

"I saw this life "pass in front of my eyes," like watching a movie. I felt others' pain, joy, sorrows." (Vincent, 1994, p. 93)

For some, life review is a negative experience:

"It was not peaceful, much baggage, much unfinished business. All things are connected. You are not your body, you are a soul; mine was in limbo. I knew I would be in limbo for a long time. I had a life review and was sent to the void." (Vincent, 1994, p. 119)

In Christianity, sometimes God is seen as Judge of the World, but more often, Jesus is seen as the Judge (Ma'sdmidn 1996). In Jesus' parable of the Rich Man and Lazarus (Luke 16:19-31), he stated that judgment began prior to him, was ongoing, and occurred immediately after death. In the Judgment of the Nations (Matthew 25:31-46), Jesus is Judge of all the world, both Christian and non-Christian. Judgment is based on good works done to the "least of these" (Matthew 25:40). Jesus taught that we must be judged, but that God is Light and goodness: God is light, and in Him there is no darkness at all (1 John 1:5).

NDErs often note that the Being of Light in the life review offers total acceptance:

"My near-death experience was before Moody's book came out. When it did, I said, Oh my God! Mine is pretty classic-just like the book. It was incredibly clear my life-going through what happened. There were figures around I did not know. The white Light was wonderful! It was just love. I knew my life would be reviewed. It was like flipping pages. I knew I had done things I was not proud of, but there was total acceptance. I wanted to stay, but I was told to go back and be loving." (Vincent 1994, p. 91)

I have already noted above that this is also true when the Being of Light is specifically identified as Jesus. This is the picture that the New Testament presents of Jesus. In the mystic Gospel of John we read: You judge by human standards. I judge no one. (John 8:15) And I, when I am lifted up from the Earth, will draw all people to myself. (John 12:32) Jesus said: "My yoke is easy, and my burden is light" (Matthew 11:30).

The following makes it clear that Jesus is an advocate for both Christians and non-Christians: My children, I am writing these things to you so that you may not sin. But if anyone does sin, we have an advocate with the Father; Jesus Christ the Righteous. He is the atoning sacrifice for our sins, and not for ours only, but also for the sins of the whole world. (1 John 2:1-2) With Jesus as Judge, no one is ever abandoned-Christian or non-Christian. Jesus told us that the Kingdom of God is not only for the pure (Matthew 5:8) but also for the impure (Matthew 15:2, Luke 18:10-14), the pagan (Matthew 15:21-28), and the heretic (Luke 10:25-37; John 4:16-30).

NDErs often feel that they judge themselves, as these quotes from three NDErs indicate:

> "You are judging yourself. You have been forgiven all your sins, but are you able to forgive yourself for not doing the things you should have done and some little cheaty things that maybe you've done in your life? This is the judgment." (Ring and Valarino, 1998, p. 167)

> "I didn't see anyone as actually judging me. It was more like I was judging myself on what I did and how that affected everyone." (Ring and Valarino, 1998, p. 167)

> "I told the Light that ... I expected him to judge me rather sternly. He said, 'Oh, no, that doesn't happen at all.' However, at my request, they then played back over the events that had occurred in my life. ... and I was the judge." (Ring and Valarino, 1998, p. 167)

Jesus clearly told us: Do not judge, so that you may not be judged. For with the judgment you make you will be judged, and the measure you give will be the measure you get. (Matthew 7:1-2) The judgment of Jesus is not based on belief in Doctrine. The test is not about correct belief, but good deeds: Not everyone who says to me, "Lord, Lord," will enter the Kingdom of Heaven, but only the one who does the will of my Father in Heaven (Matthew 7:21). Good deeds will be rewarded: For the Son of Man is to come with his angels in the glory of his Father, and then he will repay everyone for what has been done. (Matthew 16:27) St. Peter reiterated: I truly understand that God shows no partiality, but in every nation, anyone who fears him and does what is right is acceptable to Him. (Acts 10:34-35) St. Paul said: For he will repay according to each one's deeds. (Romans 2:6) For God shows no partiality. (Romans 2:11) St. John of Patmos wrote: And the dead were judged according to their works as recorded in the books. (Revelation 20:12)

Hell Is Not Permanent

The experience of Hell has been recorded in NDEs since the beginning of modern research (Richie and Sherrill, 1978). In current near-death research terminology, these are called "frightening" NDEs.

In religious terms, the place of punishment is called variously "Hell," "Hades," "Limbo," "Purgatory," "Gehenna," and "Eternal Punishment." Modern day near-death researchers have about as many types of frightening NDEs (Atwater, 1992; Greyson and Bush, 1992; Rommer, 2000) as the ancient and medieval authors had categories of Hell (Zaleski, 1987).

Often in the NDE, accounts of Hell are not permanent:

> "I was in Hell ... I cried up to God, and it was by the power of God and the mercy of God that I was permitted to come back." (Rommer 2000, p 42)

> "God, I am not ready, please help me ... I remember when I screamed (this) an arm shot out of the sky and grabbed my hand and at the last second I was kept from falling off the end of the funnel, the lights flashing; and the heat was really something." (Greyson and Bush, 1992, p.100)

If Hell is not permanent, one might wonder why Jesus said the "goats" will endure "eternal punishment" (Matthew 25:46). Universalist scholar Thomas Talbott noted that the Greek word for "forever" is better understood as "that which pertains to an age" (1997, pp. 86 92). For example, when Jonah was swallowed by the great fish, he "went down to the land whose bars closed on me forever" (Jonah 2:6).

However, the story ended when Jonah was released by God from his bondage after just three days. In other instances-his parable of the unforgiving servant (Matthew 18:34-35) and his descriptions of a prisoner's fate (Matthew 5:25-26, Luke 12:59)-Jesus indicated that punishment is not eternal but lasts only until one's entire debt is paid (Matthew 18:34). The following are classic passages supporting Christian Universalism (Howe, 1993, pp 34-35): For Christ also suffered for sins once and for all, the righteous for the unrighteous, in order to bring you to God. He was put to death in the flesh, but made alive in the Spirit in which also he went and made a proclamation to the spirits in prison, who in former times did not obey. (1 Peter 3:18-20) For this reason the Gospel was proclaimed even to the dead, so that though they had been judged in the flesh as everyone is, they might live in the Spirit as God does. (1 Peter 4:6) It appears from NDE accounts that Jesus is still rescuing people from Hell!

Universal Salvation

According to Christian Universalism, in the end, we will all be united with God. Two of Jesus' most poignant parables proclaim Universal Salvation. In Matthew, God (the Good Shepherd) sought and saved the lost sheep; the sheep did not return to the flock of its own accord. The parable ends, "So it is not the will of your Father in Heaven that one of these little ones should be lost" (Matthew 18:14). In the story of the Prodigal Son (Luke 15:11-32), the returning son did not ask to be a member of the family, but for a job as his father's servant. It was God (the father) who took him back into the family. The father was the character with the active role. People often have difficulty with this story because they wrongly identify with the good son and not with the father. Considering how much human parents love their own children, the story puts some perspective on how much God, who is all good, loves each of us.

This theme is echoed in the mystic Gospel of John: I have other sheep that do not belong to this fold, and I must bring them also, and they will listen to my voice. So there will be one flock, one shepherd. (John 10:16) And I, when I am lifted up from the earth, will draw all people to myself. (John 12:32)

Universal salvation is reiterated in numerous writings of the other Apostles: When all things are subjected to him then the Son himself will also be subjected to the one who put all things in subjection under him, so that God may be all in all. (1 Corinthians 15:28) For to this end we toil and struggle, because we have our hope set on the living God, who is the Savior of all people, especially of those who believe. (1 Timothy 4:10) And the Holy Spirit also testifies to us, for after saying, "This is the covenant I will make with them after those days, says the Lord: I will put my laws in their hearts and I will write them on their minds," he also adds: "I will remember their sins and their lawless deeds no more." Where there is forgiveness of these, there is no longer any offering for sin. (Hebrews 10:15-18) He has made known to us the mystery of his will, according to his good pleasure that he set forth in Christ, as a plan for the fullness of time, to gather up all things in him, things in heaven and things on earth. (Ephesians 1:9-10) For the grace of God has appeared, bringing salvation to all. (Titus 2:11)

Aftereffects

One of the most profound aspects of the NDE is its aftereffects (Greyson, 2000). Experiences of God change and affirm lives, and sometimes this represents a "soft" change:

> "It took some time for me to realize I was consumed with an insatiable thirst for knowledge. Dr. Pat Fenske wrote in the June, 1991, *Vital Signs* newsletter that individuals shift to a higher level of consciousness. This I can relate to 100 percent and this has enabled me to understand why I look at things from an entirely different perspective than most people." (Vincent, 1994, p. 109)

> "Why did this experience change me so greatly? Why am I convinced that this was the most real thing that ever happened to me when logic and common sense dictate it wasn't? Why so many unexplained events since then? ... The experience left me a changed person but not knowing why, full of questions and still seeking answers." (Vincent, 1994, p. 113)

In some cases, the changes following an NDE are dramatic- as life changing as St. Paul's mystical religious vision of Jesus that transformed him from a persecutor of Christians to an Evangelist for Jesus (1 Corinthians 15:3-8; Galatians 1:13-16). That kind of powerful effect occurred in the life of art professor Howard Storm, who, after his encounter with Jesus during his NDE, abandoned his atheism and became a Christian minister. Storm related that when he began to pray, his NDE changed from a Hellish experience to a positive, loving one: "Simply stated, I knew God loved me" (Ring and Valarino, 1998, p. 292).

Summary

Like NDEs, deathbed visions (Osis and Haraldsson, 1977) and after-death communications (Kircher, 1995) point to an afterlife. But NDEs, like mystical religious experiences throughout the ages (Argyle, 2000; James, 1901/1958), are especially rich in insights as to the nature of God. NDEs, like other mystical religious experiences, both complement and continue the testimony of that great repository of Western mystical experience, the Bible.

God's love is greater than we imagine or than we can imagine-this is the testimony of the prophets, sages, saints, mystics, and ordinary people throughout the ages who have shared with us their incomparable sense of Oneness with God and God's unconditional love for us all. Truly God is with us always and, in time, "All flesh shall see the salvation of God" (Luke 3:6).

CHAPTER 11

An Eighteenth Century Near-Death Experience: The Case of George de Benneville

~

(Note this chapter was co-authored by John C. Morgan, D. Min., Reading Area Community College, Reading, PA)
Near-death experiences were rarely recorded prior to modern resuscitation techniques, but there is no doubt they have occurred since the dawn of humanity. In his *Republic*, the ancient Greek philosopher and educator Plato told the story of Er, a man who revived on his funeral pyre and recounted his near-death experience (NDE) (Plato, fourth century B.C.). In the first century, Plutarch recounted the story of Thespesius of Soli who died of a blow to the head but revived during his funeral three days later (Plutarch, first century). In the sixth century, St. Gregory the Great told the story of a man named Stephen who died but came back to life before his body could be embalmed (Gregory the Great, sixth century).

The eighth century English theologian and scholar the Venerable Bede described the near-death experience of a man named Cunningham (aka Drythelm) who "rose from the dead" in 696 A.D. (Bede, eighth century). In his *Ecclesiastical History*, Bede also included two deathbed visions with similar themes. All these accounts stressed the necessity of living a righteous life in order to avoid punishment in the afterlife. Plato did not indicate Er's reputation, but Plutarch stated that Thespesius had fallen into living a less-than-sterling life, Gregory wrote that Stephen's character was mixed, and Bede noted that Cunningham became more religious and entered a monastery after his NDE.

Despite our fascination with these and other examples from ancient and medieval literature and the fact that they sound similar to modern NDE accounts, they are of little use to the modern near-death researcher. One of the most essential criteria for modern near-death research is that the account be an autobiographical or "first-hand" telling of the experience. In her analysis of medieval and modern accounts of otherworld journeys, Carol Zaleski noted, "we cannot simply peel away the literary wrapper and put our hand on an unembellished event. Even when a vision actually did occur, it is likely to have been re-worked many times before being recorded" (Zaleski, 1987, pp. 86–88). She suggested, for example, that the Church would have been eager to insure that these accounts did not contradict "truth" as defined by Church doctrine.

Before the advent of modern medicine and social sciences, there was little value placed on reporting events objectively. This was true for most mystical religious experience in general and near-death experiences in particular. Not until the end of the nineteenth century was organized research into these fields initiated by the British Society for Psychical Research and, subsequently, its American counterpart.

Against this suspicious background of NDEs interpreted through historians and theologians, we are fortunate to have one eighteenth century NDE account that would meet the standards of modern researchers.

In 1741, George de Benneville wrote his first-person NDE account. By examining his life and reputation, we hope to show that his NDE can be accepted as authentic and credible.

The Life of George de Benneville

George de Benneville (1703–1793) was a physician and lay minister in Europe and an advocate of the doctrine of Universal Salvation that, in the end of time, all creatures will be restored to what he called "happiness and holiness." He brought the spirit of German Pietist communities to the new world, principally in Pennsylvania and New Jersey, but he made frequent journeys to the Southern states.

The youngest of nine children born to Huguenot refugees, de Benneville was born and brought up in the British royal court in London, his father being a nobleman from Normandy. His godmother was Queen Anne. After growing up in England, he traveled to France and eventually settled in Germany, where he had his near-death experience at the age of 36, and from whence he immigrated to America in the second quarter of the eighteenth century, arriving in Philadelphia, but eventually settling and marrying in what is now Berks County, Pennsylvania. He built there a large house that contained a schoolroom for both immigrants and Native American children, a large room used by many religious groups, and a space for his medical practice. He learned and used many herbal remedies from tribes in the area, some of whom often would camp outside his house. He also assisted in the first German language edition of the Bible published in the United States, and put the Bible passages that justified Universal Salvation in red type.

De Benneville believed that there was an essential unity behind every appearance of religious diversity. Thus he was able to incorporate into his medical practice Native American remedies and even some of their symbols and language. In 1757 he and his family moved near Philadelphia, where he continued his medical practice while opening an apothecary shop. He treated the wounded of both sides at the Battle of Germantown in 1777 and even permitted British troops to be buried in his family plot. He died of a stroke in 1793 (De Benneville, 1804; Morgan, 1995, pp 28–33).

The Near-Death Experience of George de Benneville

This is de Benneville's NDE in his own words. The spelling and punctuation are left in their original form.

"I felt myself die by degrees, and exactly at midnight I was separated from my body, and saw the people occupied in washing it, according to the custom of the country. I had a great desire to be freed from the sight of my body, and immediately I was drawn up as in a cloud, and beheld great wonders where I passed, impossible to be written or expressed. I quickly came to a place which appeared to my eyes as a level plain, so extensive that my sight was not able to reach its limits, filled with all sorts of delightful fruit trees, agreeable to behold, and which sent forth such fragrant odours that all the air was filled as with incense. In this place I found that I had two guardians, one at my right hand and the other at my left, exceeding beautiful beyond expression, whose boundless friendship and love seemed to penetrate through all my inward parts. ... They had wings and resembled angels, having shining bodies and white garments. He that was at my right hand came before me, and said, "My dear soul and my dear brother, take courage, the most holy trinity hath favored you to be comforted with an everlasting and universal consolation, by discovering to you how, and in what manner, he will restore all his creatures without exception, to the praise of his glory, and their eternal salvation; and you shall be witness of this, and shall rejoice in singing and triumph with all the children of God, therefore as a reward for the friendship and love that you have born for your neighbours, on whose accounts you had many extreme griefs, and shed many tears, which God himself, who shall turn all your griefs to exceeding great gladness.' Then he took his place at my right hand. After that the second guardian who was at my left hand appeared before me, and spoke thus; 'My dear soul, my dear brother, be of good cheer, thou shalt be strengthened and comforted after your griefs with an universal and eternal consolation. ... You must be prepared to pass through the seven habitations of the damned; be of good courage and prepare yourself to feel something of their sufferings, but be turned inward deeply during the time, and you shall thereby be preserved.' Then he took his place at my left hand; immediately we were lifted up in the air, and sometimes after we arrived in a dark obscure place, where nothing but weeping, lamentation, and gnashing of teeth, could be understood. A dreadful place, as being the repository of all sorts of damned souls, under condemnation with the torments, pains, griefs and sufferings which their sins had merited, for each one had his works to follow him in death. All iniquities and sins were reduced to seven classes or habitations: there was an eternal confusion there, that which one made, the other destroyed.

The duellist, in his fire of anger, burns against his enemy, and they pass as a flame and firebrand of hell, one through the other. You might see fornicators, idolaters, adulterers, thieves, the covetous, drunkards, slanderers, ravishers, etc., each laboring and being employed with his sins and iniquities. One might also see all kind of conditions of men, divines, deputies, controvertors, advocates, judges, lawyers, and in a word one might discover whatsoever any of them had done upon earth. In each habitation I discovered that those who were abased and that appeared sorrowful for their sins, were separated from the others of seven habitations of the damned, where I knew one I had been acquainted with upon earth. I discovered also that he had an habitation among the damned, and that they were able to see the elect from that habitation where he was, but were not able to pass through because there was a great gulph between them, so that all are obliged to dwell where they are. It is impossible to describe my condition, as I had great compassion towards the sufferers, inasmuch as I had part of their sufferings.

After we had passed through we were lifted up some distance from the place, where we reposed ourselves; and a messenger was sent to us, who watered or refreshed us as with a river of pleasure, saying, eat, my beloved, and drink, my friends, to refresh yourselves after all your toils and pains; my dear soul, and my dear brother, (addressing himself to me) the most holy trinity always works wonders in all times within his poor creatures without exception, and he will order for a time, and half a time, that you shall return into your earthly tabernacle, to publish and to proclaim to the people of the world an universal gospel, that shall restore in its time all the human species without exception to its honor and to the glory of its most holy trinity. ... Hallelujah. Beholding the messenger attentively, I discovered that he had a most glorious body, dressed in a robe whiter than snow, filled with the most exalted love and friendship, joined with the deepest humility which penetrated me through and through, and suddenly there was heard a great multitude of the heavenly host, and the messenger said, as he flew to join the same, with a sweet voice – 'Holy, holy is the Lord God Almighty, who was, and is, and who is to come.' The multitude were innumerable, and there was one who surpassed in grandeur, brightness, beauty, majesty, magnificence and excellence, all the others; even the son of the living God, being the brightness of his glory and the express image of his person, and upholding all things by the word of his power, when he had by himself purged our sins, sat down at the right hand of the majesty on high. As the multitude approached the glory caused us to fall down, and to adore in spirit and in truth the son of the living God, who marched in the midst of the multitude.

After they had passed us, we were lifted up, and caused to follow them, for the air carried us the way they went, in a different manner than before. Oh! the wonders of our God! When we arrived in the place of the seven habitations of the damned, we could perceive no more darkness, obscurity, pain, torments, lamentations, afflictions, nor gnashing of teeth. All were still and quiet, and an agreeable sweetness appeared through the whole. Then all the heavenly host shouted with one voice and said, 'An eternal and everlasting deliverance, an eternal and everlasting restoration, universal and everlasting restitution of all things.' Then all the multitude adored the most holy trinity, and sang the song of the Lamb, even the song of the triumph for the victory gained by him, in the most harmonious manner. And at the end, all the multitude being upon their knees, said with a loud voice, 'Great and marvelous are thy works, O Lord, God Almighty, just and true are thy ways. Oh! King of Saints.' Presently they passed through the seven habitations of the damned and a multitude were delivered from each, and being clothed in white robes, they followed the heavenly host, praising and glorifying the most high for their deliverance; one might know them amongst the others: they all retired by a different way than that which they came.

The messenger then came and conducted us into a most wonderful place, and ordered my two guardians to conduct me into five celestial mansions, where the Lord's elect abide; and then to reconduct me to dwell yet a time, and half a time in my earthly habitation, and to preach to the lower world the universal everlasting gospel; and that the most holy trinity hath a pure universal love towards all the human race, without exception, and to each one in particular; then turning himself towards me he said, my dear soul, my dear brother, thou shalt be favored of the most holy trinity, to be conducted by thy guardians, who shall never leave thee; when thou shall have need of their counsel, thou needest but to call them, and they shall be day and night present at thy service; they shall conduct thee into five of the heavenly mansions at this time, where thou shalt partake in a certain degree, of the celestial glory as much as thy spirit shall be able to receive, as not being yet sanctified and purified sufficiently, and then thou shall be reconducted into thine earthly tabernacle, for a time and half a time and shall preach to the lower world the universal everlasting gospel, and that the most holy trinity hath a pure universal love towards all the human race without exception, and towards each one in particular. The fountain of grace bless and preserve thee, and cause his face to shine upon and in thee, and enlighten thine understanding both in time and in eternity, Amen. Our knees bending of their own accord, he laid his hand upon my head, and blessed me, and immediately took wing and swiftly fled away.

After that, my guardian conducted me into five celestial habitations, where I discovered many wonders. Some had greater brightness, glory, and majesty than others, and, as the places were, so were the inhabitants; some were clothed in garments whiter then snow; others had transparent bodies, and others again had white bodies resembling crystal. It is impossible to express these things. They were moved by boundless burning love, rising up and then plunging themselves into the deepest humility; all their motions were penetrating, being filled with love and friendship. ... Their actions and manners are strengthened and animated with brightness, being filled with light as with the rays of the sun; it was the fire of heavenly love, which by inflaming all their hearts, causes them all to burn in the same spirit. They have no need of any way of speaking there, but the language and motions of eternal and universal love without words for their actions, their motions speak more than all words. I was then conducted into five habitations of the elect. At the first, a great multitude came before us with songs to the honor and glory of the most high, and of the victory gained over the damned. They received us with triumph, great zeal, love and friendship, saluting us with profound humility, and conducting us into a large room; there was a great table covered and furnished with all sorts of fruit, not only pleasant to behold, but also exceedingly delicious to the taste.

In the meantime while we were taking our repast, the celestial multitudes formed songs, and sang psalms of praise and thanksgiving to the most holy trinity. After that we were conducted into all the five celestial habitations (that I was to see) where I saw many wonders, impossible to describe. First, many thrones lifted up of inexpressible beauty and magnificence; upon one of these thrones I beheld the royal high priest, surrounded with exceeding great brightness, and clothed in most excellent majesty, being employed in kind intercession before his father, for all the human species, pleading the sufficiency of his blood-shedding to deliver and sanctify a thousand such worlds as ours. All the elect, with the heavenly spirits, joined their intercession with that of their high priest, the only chief king, being reconcilers, saviors, and restorers in the same spirit. This mutual intercession appeared like incense ascending on high into the sanctuary of the Lord. Over against the throne I discovered Adam with Eve, rejoicing in the only mediator between God and men, and adoring together the most holy trinity for the deliverance of their children out of the great miseries and eternal condemnation into which their sin and fall had brought them, and upon their bended knees adoring the only mediator for the intercession he makes in behalf of mankind. Also I beheld a multitude of spirits flying and enflamed with the fire of heavenly love, while we adored, humbled in nothingness, rendering our religious homage to the most high for his intercession and the deliverance of all mankind.

Then my guardian, who was at my right hand, coming before me, said thus, 'Dear soul, my dear brother, do you see these spirits flying, who are vanished in the spirit of love and gratitude, humbled and self-annihilated as it were, adoring before the throne of grace, and praying the saviour for the intercessions he made for them. These are lately delivered from the infernal prisons; it is from them that the tincture of the blood of Jesus Christ hath been shed even to the last drop, notwithstanding they had dwelt a long time shut up in the place of the damned, under the power of the second death, and have passed thro' many agonies, pains and tribulations. ...' Upon that, I perceived that Adam and Eve approached, and Adam spoke to me after his manner. ... 'My dear brother, rejoice with universal and eternal joy, as you are favored with the heavenly visions! it is in this manner that our adorable royal high priest, mediator, and intercessor, shall restore all my descendents to the glory of our God, and their eternal and universal salvation for the kingdom of eternal love hath power sufficient to draw all mankind out of their bondage, and to exclaim and say; O death, where is thy sting, etc. But my dear brother, this love of our God in Jesus Christ, by the power of his holy spirit, shall not only gain the victory over all the human species, but also surmount or overflow the kingdom of Satan entirely, with all the principalities of the fallen angels, and shall bring them back in their first glory, which they have had in the beginning. I will make all things new, said the Lord of hosts, and the end shall return into its beginning, O my Lord and my God, what great wonders hast thou caused to pass before mine eyes! Who am I, O my God, dust and ashes, an ungrateful and rebellious creature, I should not dare to lift mine eyes towards the heavens if the blood of Jesus Christ thy son did not plead for me. My soul rejoices and is glad, she shouts for joy; O my God, whom I adore, love, and respect; before whom I desire to be without ceasing, self-annihilated at thy feet. O my God and my love, the seraphims and cherubims burning with the fire of thy heavenly love, adore and honor thee; give me thy grace also, O my God, that I may be consumed before thee, while I sing the majesty, glory, and the memory of God, who hath created and redeemed me. I would praise him incessantly, not in shadow or figure, but in reality and truth. I would continue devoted to thee, and always be swallowed up in the ocean of love without a wish to leave it.'

Being in this manner conducted into five celestial habitations, I discovered many mysteries, saw many miracles, and beheld the wonders of the most holy trinity among the children, the elect, and heavenly inhabitants, and perceiving how some surpassed others in brightness, light, splendor, majesty, friendship, love, humiliation, and self-abasement, concerning of which things my tongue is too feeble to speak, and my pen to write. I adore the marvelous ways of my God, with all the happy spirits. Many thrones, palaces, edifices, temples, and buildings were erected in all parts, with fruit trees intermixed, rivers of pleasure gliding along through the celestial land, which appeared like a garden of heaven, even the paradise of God. It is the court of the King of Kings, and Lord of Lords, which the eye has not seen nor the ear heard, and which the hearts of men have not received. It is the celestial globe where the New Jerusalem, or Mount Sion, is placed, where the bosom of Abraham is; where the sufferers who came out of their tribulations are refreshed, and rejoice forgetting all their miseries; being come out of their purifications, they are made to rejoice in Sion; O magnificent globe! O thou city of the Great God! stately city of this place! Where shall a mortal find convenient phrases to lift out a little of thy glory and splendor? It is the glory and magnificence of the most holy trinity, where God is pleased to manifest himself in his pomp and beauty. The blessed angels have their employment in serving God; they compose the court of the Great King. O my God, I am not able to express that which penetrates me, of the grandeur, magnificence, splendor, pomp and majesty of thy dwellings, or of the inhabitants in those transparent places, hallelujah and victory for ever. ... AMEN.

Then my guardian took me up, and reconducted me to the house from whence I came, where I perceived the people assembled, and discovering my body in the coffin, I was reunited with the same, and found myself lodged within my earthly tabernacle, and coming to myself, I knew my dear brother Marsey, and many others, who gave me an account of my being twenty-five hours in the coffin, and seventeen hours before they put me in the coffin, which altogether made forty-two hours; to me they seemed as many years; beginning then to preach the universal gospel, I was presently put in prison, but soon set at liberty again. I visited all my brethren, preaching the gospel and taking leave of them all, because that my God and Sovereign Good called me to go to America and preach the gospel there. I took my departure for the same in the thirty-eighth year of my age, and it is forty-one years since I first arrived here. The twenty-eighth of July next, 1782, I shall be 79 years of age. Blessed be the name of the Lord forever."

The Visions of George de Benneville

The NDE is considered to be one category of mystical experience with an easily identifiable "trigger," that of dying briefly. Other mystical experiences include visionary experiences, out-of-body experiences, deathbed visions, and after-death communications. Modern studies have shown that about 40 percent of the populations of developed countries have had mystical experiences (Hay, 1987; Wood, 1989). There is some evidence that the number increases to as high as 65 percent when subjects are interviewed personally rather than being queried by written questionnaire (Hardy, 1979).

A legitimate question often asked is how we know these people are not simply delusional. Social scientists have now accumulated enough data to state that five percent of the population experiences psychosis in their lifetime (Wood and Wood, 1999). In comparing the relatively small percentage of psychotic persons to the number reporting mystical experience, the mystics clearly predominate. While visionary experience is more commonly identified with mental illness than non-visionary mystical experience, research in the nineteenth century, as well as research in the twentieth century using random samples, showed the majority of persons experiencing hallucinations were not psychotic (Bentall, 2000; West 1995). In reviewing de Benneville's personal history carefully, there is no evidence that his visions were the result of psychosis.

In addition to his NDE, de Benneville had visionary experiences. His first vision occurred as a teenager while he was changing his shirt at a ball. In his words, he "fell into a fainting fit and had a vision of myself burning as a firebrand in hell" (1804, p. 7). After an interval of 15 months, he had a vision of Jesus revealing to him that his sins were forgiven and that all people would receive salvation. When he began to talk about this vision to others, his story was brought to the attention of French Calvinist ministers who were in exile with him. He said, "They held to predestination, and I held to the restoration of all souls" (1804, p. 12). He was cast out of the Calvinist church, his own personal religious experience having trumped church authority. As we still find today, persons whose mystical religious experience is accepted by their church community tend to remain within it, while those whose congregations condemn them exit rather than deny the truth of their own experience.

De Benneville's next religious experience was at age 17 years when he heard an internal voice "calling me to go to France to preach the

Gospel" (1804, p. 13). His fourth experience, which occurred during the time he was preaching on the European continent, was a vision of heaven where people were worshiping God. He reported falling ill in his late 30s and suffering a high fever from "a consumptive disorder" (1804, p. 18). He again had visions of a fine plain filled with fruit trees and inhabitants who were "clothed in garments white as snow" (1804, p. 19). This is the only one of his visionary accounts considered to be compromised because of the presence of fever. He subsequently died and had a NDE, as related above.

Judgment or Life Review in World Religions

De Benneville's NDE is similar to many pre-modern NDEs in which the person died but revived near the time of burial. The theological idea that humans face Judgment of Deeds, often called a life review in NDE accounts, dates to ancient Egypt. It appeared in the instruction for Merikare more than 4,100 years ago (Assmann, 2005). Coexisting with this Judgment were the *Pyramid Texts* and the *Book of the Dead*, which provided the deceased with magical instruction to insure a positive outcome (Spence, 1990/1915). We do not claim that these Egyptian texts were based on NDEs or mystical religious experiences; they were simply Egyptian theology with a familiar "ring." In Zoroastrianism, judgment is determined by weighing good deeds against bad deeds. Those who do not measure up are purified in Hell until they "shape up" (Vincent, 1999, pp. 46–47), after which all are saved.

In both Plato's and Plutarch's accounts, the NDErs witnessed Judgment, Heaven, and Hell; after a period of time, the deceased were reincarnated (Plato, 1892/fourth century B.C.; Plutarch, 1918/first century). These Greco-Roman accounts echoed the theology of the Eastern religions – Hindu, Buddhist, Sikh, and Jain (Bhattacharji, 1987; Evans-Wentz, 1957; Merh, 1996; Nigosian, 2000; Vincent, 2005). In the Hindu religion and its derivatives, there is Judgment, followed by an intermediate state of Heaven or Hell that is not permanent; reincarnation follows for all except the few who are pure. Reincarnation has only begun to be studied objectively, but Ian Stevenson and Jim Tucker at the University of Virginia Medical School and their colleagues have gathered 2,500 contemporary cases suggestive of reincarnation (Tucker, 2005).

In the Christian account of Gregory the Great, a man named Stephen was taken before the heavenly judge and had his case dismissed because of "mistaken identity." Curiously, his neighbor died during the same hour, also with the name of Stephen (Gregory the Great, sixth century). This kind of error is commonly reported in Hindu NDEs (Pasricha and Stevenson, 1986). While he was dead, Stephen found himself on a bridge with Heaven on one side and Hell below the bridge. He observed that the unjust would slip off the bridge and fall into Hell (Gregory the Great, sixth century). This kind of "bridge" imagery is also present in Zoroastrianism and Shiite Islam (Moulton, 1980). In Bede's account, the Christian NDEr was shown Heaven, Hell, and purgatory (Bede, eighth century). As mentioned before, the Medieval Church often edited accounts to conform to official dogma. Gregory the Great admitted as much when he wrote, "God allows some souls to return to their bodies shortly after death, so that the sight of hell may at last teach them to fear eternal punishments in which words alone could not make them believe" (Gregory the Great, sixth century).

From Judgment to Universal Salvation

In de Benneville's NDE, we have a first-hand account from a reliable individual. In it, he asserted the primary tenet of Universalism, that after purification in Hell, all will be saved. De Benneville's NDE reinforced his earlier vision that caused his abrupt change in theology from Calvinist predestination to Christian Universalism. De Benneville's NDE conformed to modern NDEs in two important aspects: NDEs are largely positive in nature, and those who initially find themselves in Hell can reverse their fortune by calling out to God (Vincent, 2003). In fact, de Benneville's account was compatible with the contemporary account of George Ritchie (1998) who recounted that in the hellish regions of his NDE, angels were trying to help those in Hell. In his vision, Ritchie was told by Jesus, "You are right, for I, Love, be lifted up, I shall draw all men [people] unto Me" (p. 44). This is virtually identical wording to the great Universalist Biblical passage of John 12:32: "and I, when I am lifted up from the earth, will draw all people to myself" (NRSV).

The first person to speak of Universal Salvation was not a Christian, but rather Zoroaster, the ancient Persian prophet of the Magi, who lived about 1200 A.D. (Vincent, 1999). Zoroaster said that God based salvation on good deeds in this life; Christian Universalism added Jesus's message of forgiveness (Matthew 6:12–15). Christian Universalism is supported by numerous verses in the Hebrew Bible and New Testament (Vincent,

2005). The earliest theological writing on Christian Universalism was that of St. Clement of Alexandria in the second century. His pupil, Origen, was Universalism's most influential theorist (Vincent, 2005).

In the seventh century, Universalism was dealt a blow when Origen's theology was condemned by the Roman Catholic Church, although it remained viable in the Churches of the East. In the West, Universalism was relegated to the realm of mystics until the Reformation (Hanson, 1899). Julian of Norwich was one of the best examples of this. Although her Universalist mystical experiences of God and Jesus were contrary to Roman Catholic doctrine, she wrote that both her experiences and Catholic teaching must be true in some sense, a "dance" that enabled her to keep in the good graces of the Catholic Church (Hick, 1999).

In the Church of the East, Universalism continued, and parts of the Universalist teachings of Theodore of Mopsuestia are still in the liturgy of the Nestorian Church today (Hanson, 1999). Christian Universalism was also found in the Chapter 60 of the *Book of the Bee*, written by the thirteenth-century bishop Solomon of Basra. With the Renaissance, there was a revival of Universalist Christianity in the West, and for a time in the nineteenth century, the Universalist Church of America was the sixth largest denomination in the United States. It survives today in the now interfaith Unitarian Universalist Association, of which Universalist Christians (like the authors) are only a small remnant. In the twenty-first century, Christian Universalism is advocated by a wide variety of Christians from post-Vatican II Catholics to Primitive Baptists (Vincent, 2005, p 5).

Discussion

De Benneville's NDE was preceded by a mystical religious experience in the form of a vision that was Universalist in nature, a theological concept completely contrary to his religious upbringing. Departing from the Calvinist view of salvation for a few "elect," de Benneville spent the remainder of his life as a minister and physician witnessing for his understanding of a God too good to condemn anyone to Eternal Hell. His reversal was as dramatic a change as that of St. Paul (I Corinthians 15:3–8; Galatians 1:13–16) who went from persecuting Christians to being one of Christianity's major evangelists.

In recent years, there has been much documentation that both mystical religious experiences and NDEs change the lives of those who have them in positive and lasting ways (Greyson, 2000; Hay, 1987). In de Benneville's autobiography, we have a credible person's account of his mystical experiences and NDE. His life reflected his belief in God's Universal, unconditional love for all.

CHAPTER 12

Zoroaster: The First Universalist

O nce upon a time, before wisdom was confined to books, Shamans of the "Great Spirit' anticipated an afterlife for their peoples. But the earliest existing expression of the Universalist idea of an afterlife where God saves ALL people can be found in the revelation of Zoroaster, Prophet of the Magi. Truly, it is one of many profound influences that Zoroaster's new religion had on the subsequent development of Judaism, Christianity, and Islam. Known as Zoroaster by the Greeks and Zardust by the Arabs, he is properly called Zarathushtra by the followers of the religion he founded. (Since he is best known in the West by the Greek name Zoroaster, that name will be used in this paper; interestingly, the Greek name "Jesus" also became favored over the Hebrew "Yeshua.")

According to the Holy Book of the Magi, Zoroaster was born in eastern Iran and lived from about 660 BCE to 583 BCE. Like Moses (who is thought to have lived between 1600 and 1200 BCE), there is virtually no corroborative historical evidence for his life outside the religious writings. Most scholars place Zoroaster's life earlier in history (as long ago as 1200-1800 BCE), mainly due to the ancient Eastern Persian language he used to compose his Hymns (Gathas). Zoroaster's parents were middle-class, and his father was probably a horse or camel trader as well as a priest. He was married and had children. His major revelations occurred at age 30 after he, like Jesus, went into the wilderness to seek God. After this experience, he was inspired to say that, "God declared to me that silent meditation is the best for attaining spiritual enlightenment" (Y43.15). The Holy Book of the Magi relates how Satan tempted him in the wilderness with a promise of a 1,000-year rule. He preached for ten years without success, after which he converted his cousin, the rest of his family, and King Vishtaspa.

Once Zoroastrianism was adopted by the kings of Persia, the religion spread throughout the Persian Empire. The Magi, who at that time were priests of the old pagan religion in western Iran, accepted and taught the new religion of Zoroaster; some believe that Zoroaster himself was a Magus of the old religion prior to his divine revelations. His Hymns to God (*Gathas*), about the length of the Gospel of Matthew, were first recited orally and eventually written into the Holy Book of the Magi (*Avesta*). We know that he was assassinated by a rival priest at the age of 77 years. While Zoroaster claimed no divinity for himself, later traditions created miraculous stories that were characteristically attached to persons held in high esteem in the ancient world. A fond tradition claims that Zoroaster laughed (instead of crying) at birth! In the religion of the Magi, humanity has free will to choose between good and evil, and we are required to be active participants with God in the eventual defeat of evil. The core beliefs are often summarized succinctly in the phrase: "Good thoughts, good words, and good deeds." Zoroaster's name for God is "Ahura Mazda" which means, "Lord of Life and Wisdom" or simply "Wise Lord." This can be compared to the literal translations of the names for God in Hebrew Scriptures: "Yahweh" which means "I AM" and "Elohim" which means "God." For Zoroaster, God is wholly good; God unconditionally and totally loves all his Creation and all humanity – always. God is not angry, jealous, or vengeful; God would never tempt humans into doing evil.

We are made of the essence of God and are cherished by God. Fasting, celibacy, and the austere life have no place in the religion of the Magi; one is simply directed to BE LIKE GOD–Do Good and Oppose Evil. (Christians may recall that in Matthew 5:48, Jesus also commands us to be like our heavenly Father.) Because all creation is sacred, it is also humanity's duty to protect creation and not defile it or pollute it. (In a very real way, Zoroaster was the first environmentalist!)

God is opposed by an evil force called "The Demon of the Lie" which Zoroaster described as "that which is not and never was"—almost as if he saw the devil as a vacuum. Satan is responsible for all death, destruction, decay, and darkness. Satan has no physical presence on Earth but does have the ability to corrupt God's creation. However, Satan is dim-witted and disorganized and can be defeated by the Good! Like Christianity, the religion of the Magi has a concept of the Holy Spirit as being the part of God that is present with us on the Earth. God is both immanent (present) and transcendent (other). It is the Holy Spirit or Mentality of God (Spenta Mainyu) that counters the Evil Spirit or Mentality (Angra Mainyu). In the words of Zoroaster: "Through his Holy Spirit and his Sovereign mind, Ahura Mazda will grant self-realization and immortality to him whose words and deeds are inspired by righteousness, moral courage and divine wisdom" (Y47.1). Both the ancient Magi and the modern followers of Zoroaster see God as Light, the oldest non- anthropomorphic conception of God. God is the light above us, around us, and within us. For Zoroaster, the contrast between light and darkness is always a metaphor for the conflict between Good and Evil. In speaking of the God of the Magi, the third-century Greek philosopher Porphyry said, "God's body is Light, and His Spirit Truth." In more modern times, Einstein saw all matter as frozen light, and physicist Stephen Hawking stated, "When you break subatomic particles down to their most elemental level, you are left with nothing but pure light." Sometimes observers of this religion from ancient to modern times have mistaken the Magi for fire worshippers because of the "eternal flame" present in all of their temples. However, the fire has never been worshiped; the flame of the fire represents LIGHT, their symbol for God.

Concepts of the afterlife in the religion of the Magi are almost identical to those of Christianity. Joseph Campbell suspects direct borrowing of the ideas of the Magi by Dante in his vivid descriptions of a multi-layered Heaven and Hell. According to Zoroaster's vision, each human soul is required to face judgment on the "Bridge of Judgment." If there is a preponderance of good deeds, the soul is allowed to pass over a wide bridge to Heaven on which the good deeds meet him or her in the form of a beautiful 15-year-old girl. The soul of the saved asks, "Who are thou, for I have never seen a young girl on Earth more beautiful or fair than thee?" In answer, the young girl replies, "I am no girl, but thy own good deeds." If the human soul contains a preponderance of evil deeds, a young girl "who has no semblance of a young girl" comes to meet it, and the soul of the damned says, "Who are thou? I have never seen a wench on Earth more ill-favored and hideous than thee." In reply, the ill-favored wench says, "I am no wench, but I am thy deeds – hideous deeds – evil thoughts, evil words, evil deeds, and evil religion." The Bridge then becomes razor narrow and the soul falls into Hell. This same razor sharp bride imagery lives on in Shiite Islam.

Unlike Dante whose Limbo is for the righteous who are not Christians, Limbo in the religion of the Magi is for those whose good deeds and bad deeds are in equal balance. The Hell of the Magi is not eternal but only a temporary detour while you "shape up" and the evil in you is purified. Zoroastrians, like other Universalists, believe God is too good to sentence humans to Eternal Hell. Some modern minimalist scholars dispute the fact that Zoroaster was a Universalist and say that Universal Salvation came into Zoroastrianism later; however, as Mary Boyce points out in *Textual Sources for the Study of Zoroastrianism*, the religion was definitely Universalist many years before Christianity when the fourth century B.C. Greek, Theopompus stated that "Zoroaster prophesies that someday there will be a resurrection of all the dead. In the end Hades shall perish and men (people) shall be happy ..."

In the religion of the Magi, the Archangels – called the "Bounteous Immortals" – are very powerful, as you can tell from their names: "The Good Mind", "Righteousness", "Divine Power", "Universal Love", "Perfection", and "Immortality." Interestingly, half are male and half are female. They were created by God and with the Angels serve as a link of communication between humanity and God. Additionally, they are manifestations of the characteristics present in men and women of good will—those that each of us needs to integrate into our lives in order to serve God. For instance, good men and women manifest the characteristics of the Archangel of the Good Mind, while evil people are beset with the Evil Mind. The Archangels have been called deities erroneously by some scholars. Some scholars maintain that Zoroaster's original conception was that of highly abstract Archangels which represent mere aspects of God. Tradition and, more importantly, followers of the modern Zoroastrian religion interpret them literally as Archangels. The Magi also believed that there were Earth Angels of which the prophet Zoroaster was one. Dr. J. J. Modi sees parallels between the Christian angel Michael and the Zoroastrian angel Mithra, as well as between the Christian angel Gabriel and the Zoroastrian angel Sraosha.

The name of Mithra may sound familiar to Westerners because of a heretical cult during Roman times that extended as far west as England. This "mystery religion" (which allowed only men) worshipped Mithra as a god, and its popularity is said to have rivaled the early Christian movement. Curiously, Mithra's birthday is December 25, a date adopted later by the Christian Church for Christmas in its effort to discourage participation in this pagan celebration. Mithra is still worshipped as a god in India. However, in the orthodox religion of the Magi, Zoroastrians consider Mithra "only" an Angel and not even an Archangel!

Sophy Burnham, author of *A Book of Angels*, credits Zoroaster with the development of the concept of angels. Before their contact with the Magi, the Hebrews often refer to the messengers of God as simply men (as in Genesis 18 when three men, one of whom is God, appear to Abraham). After their contact with the Magi, Judaism and later Christianity and Islam have a well-developed system of Archangels and Angels.

Both a spiritual afterlife of the soul and a physical resurrection at the end of time are concepts of Zoroaster. Humanity can fall prey to evil, but after "purification" in Hell, ALL are saved at the end of time. When the victory over evil is complete, the end of time will come where nothing ever dies or decays, and there is no darkness – only LIGHT.

In the spirit of Universalism, Zoroaster tells of future Saviors possibly coming from different nations: "Indeed such shall be the Saviors of the countries who follow the call of Duty by good thoughts. Because of their deeds inspired by righteousness in accord with your command, O Mazda, they certainly have been marked out as smiters of wrath (Y48.12)."

One ongoing issue in Zoroastrianism present since antiquity is the debate between those who interpret Zoroaster's understanding of God as "ethical dualism" (monotheism) and those who maintain the concept of "cosmic dualism" (God and Satan co-exist). Although Zoroaster was very sure that God is wholly good and that man is free to choose good or evil, his teachings were unclear about the source of evil in the world. That is, if God the Creator is all good, where does evil come from? Those supporting ethical dualism (monotheism) would answer that evil originates in the mind of humanity and is the byproduct of creation; because the Universe is incomplete and unfinished, there is a capacity to alter the status quo. That is why humanity must be active in helping God to overcome evil. The Zoroastrian scholar and modern-day believer, Prof. Farhang Mehr, sees Zoroaster as a pure monotheist who taught ethical dualism rather than cosmic dualism.

Throughout the long history of this religion, the concept of cosmic dualism has been more widely accepted; that is, a belief that good comes from God and that evil comes from Satan, although God is Eternal and Satan is not. Interestingly, this same concept of cosmic dualism is used throughout the New Testament by both Jesus and St. Paul, although the monotheism of Christianity is never doubted. Satan is a very real and powerful being to Jesus; he is tempted by Satan in the three Synoptic Gospels (Mt 4:1-11, Mk 1:12 -13, Lk 4:1-13). He asks, "How can Satan cast out Satan? If a kingdom is divided against itself, that kingdom cannot stand" (Mt.12: 25-26, Mk 3:23-24, Lk 11:17-18). In Ephesians 6:11, Paul writes, "Put on the whole armor of God so that you may be able to stand against the wiles of the Devil." The proponents of cosmic dualism feel comfortable with modern-day "Process Theology" which expresses the idea that God cannot bestow free will and remain all powerful. A concept in modern physics that may reinforce the reality of cosmic dualism is that "a little chaos" is present in every atom of the Universe.

The God of the Magi is Universal, and Zoroaster was the first to proclaim this truth. In the words of the Persian (and Zoroastrian) King Darius, "I am King of all the Nations by the will of God." In the words of Zoroaster, God is supreme: "When I held you in my very eyes then I realized you in my mind, O Mazda, as the first and also the last for all eternity, as the Father of good thoughts, as the Creator of righteousness and Lord over the actions of life (Y31.8)."

Although the Persian Empire fell to Alexander the Great (331BCE), the Magi continued to be very influential throughout the Middle East and the Western World, and the religion of the Magi continued as the primary religion in the Middle East until the Moslem conquest (642 CE). The Magi were prized as teachers of great wisdom and power, and Zoroaster remained a highly respected figure. Of course, Zoroastrian ideas have been enormously important to subsequent religious thought. Many scholars contend that it was Zoroaster's cursing of the Hindu gods that initiated the break between the religious approaches of the East (Hindu, Buddhism) and those of the West (Judaism, Christianity, Islam). In the Dead Sea Scrolls of the Essenes, the imagery of the "Sons of Light" and "Sons of Darkness" is a direct borrowing from the Religion of the Magi. Six hundred years after the Moslem conquest, the Sufi Mystic, Attar of Nishopur, wrote, "we are the Eternal Magi, we are not Muslims." The Cypress slender Minister of Wine in the *Rubaiyat of Omar Khayyam* is a Magi. Omar Khayyam once said he wore the belt of a Magi because he was ashamed of his Islam. Zoroaster taught that God loves us all and that, after evil is finally defeated, ALL humanity will be saved at the end of time, although those whose bad deeds outweigh their good deeds will need to be "purified" in Hell before joining God in Heaven.

The following example illustrates the views of Zoroaster concerning Universal Salvation:

"If you understand these laws of happiness and pain, which Mazda has ordained, O mortal men,

(there is) a long period of punishment for the wicked and reward for the pious *but thereafter eternal joy shall reign forever* (Y30.11, emphasis added)."

CHAPTER 13

Omar Khayyam: Sufi Universalist

O mar Khayyam is one of my heroes. I have read translations of his poem, the *Rubaiyat,* hundreds of times over the past 50 years. Amazingly, each repetition still brings some fresh insight! Rubai means "quatrain," a four-line stanza in which there are two sets of rhyming lines. (In this article, the numbered stanzas are from E. H. Whinfield's second translation.) The *Rubaiyat* is a collection of quatrains written over a period of many years by Omar Khayyam, a Sufi mystic living in the late eleventh and early twelfth centuries. Within Omar's poetry, I recognize a person much like myself: someone unable to be an orthodox believer but too optimistic to be agnostic! His verses reflect the impossibility of certainty in religion, philosophy, or science; he questions the theological tenants of all religions. Ultimately, he was simply a lover of God. He believed his own mystical experiences which became the basis of his faith:

#287 Although the creeds number some seventy-three, I hold with none but that of loving Thee; What matter faith, unfaith, obedience, sin? Thou'rt all we need, the rest is vanity.

One of Omar's most important theological truths is that God is ONE. His mystical experiences convinced him that there is ONE TRUTH behind all the world's religions:

> #63 Hearts with the light of love illumined well, Whether in mosque or synagogue they dwell, Have their names written in the book of love, Unvexed by hopes of heaven or fears of Hell.

Omar had the good fortune to live in Nishapur, a prosperous city on the Silk Road, at a time when the Moslems had ruled Iran for 500 years. Significantly, a large minority of followers of the Zoroastrian religion whom Omar called "Magians" still resided in this area. He was also acquainted with the beliefs of smaller religious minorities in the region—Jews and Christians, as well as Buddhist travelers. In his poem, he shows respect for all of these religions. He recognizes that ALL yearn for God—that all are seeking the ONE:

> #34 Pagodas, just as mosques, are homes of prayer, 'Tis prayer that church-bells chime unto the air, Yea, Church and Ka'ba, Rosary and Cross Are all but divers tongues of worldwide prayer.

While any monotheist may become a Sufi, they are most often associated with Islam. Ultra- orthodox Sufis may choose to obey Islamic law but add some mystical component. Other Sufis (like Omar) view Islamic law much the way Jesus viewed the ritualistic Jewish Law – that it is more important to obey the spirit than the letter of the law. Consequently, Omar was admired by some Sufis who used his poem as a teaching tool but, like Jesus, he was cursed by those who were victims of his barbed criticisms of religious hypocrisy. In another behavior reminiscent of Jesus, Omar openly associated with sinners. Both believed that God wants us to speak, act, and live from our hearts.

> #368 Hear now Khayyam's advice, and bear in mind, Consort with revelers, though they be maligned, Cast down the gates of abstinence and prayer, Yea, drink, and even rob, but oh! Be kind!

Omar was a scientist, astronomer, and mathematician. Everyone who has ever taken algebra has been taught his binomial theorem! As an astronomer, he revised the Persian calendar to be as accurate as our present Georgian calendar, but he did so 500 years earlier and without the use of telescopes! Many people have attempted to translate the *Rubaiyat*; some translations are academic, literal, and "dry as a bone," while others are simply paraphrases. At one time or another, I have owned 21 different translations. Probably the best-known one is that of Edmund Fitzgerald who first published in 1859 but subsequently made 4 other translations over the next 30 years. It is Fitzgerald's version of this familiar verse that falls so easily on our ears:

"A loaf of bread, a jug of wine, and thou, a book of poems beneath the bough."

However, my favorite translator is E. H. Whinfield because of his effort to balance the meaning of the poems with a pleasing rhythm. While keeping the words as literally accurate as possible, he takes enough "poetic license" to insure that the poems remain beautiful when read aloud. Whinfield made three translations of the *Rubaiyat*. His second translation was selected by Joseph Campbell for the epic series, *The Masks of God*, so I assume that Campbell favored this translation too.

Contrary to what you may have assumed when you were exposed to the *Rubaiyat* as an adolescent, the poem is NOT about living for the moment without regard for tomorrow! Omar does not advocate irresponsibility, but he does want to persuade people to BE ALIVE IN THE MOMENT – to enjoy what we have today –NOW! He is addressing those who live "in the past" or those who imagine that happiness is not possible until some imagined goal is achieved or current problem resolved:

#30 To-day is thine to spend, but not tomorrow, Counting on morrows breedeth naught but sorrow; Oh! Squander not this breath that heaven hath lent thee Nor make too sure another breath to borrow!

Omar's respect for the insight of other religions includes the "middle way" of Buddha and Lao Tzu which asserts that it is best to live modestly – shunning poverty or wealth:

#168 Let him rejoice who has a loaf of bread, A little nest wherein to lay his head; Is slave to none and no man slaves for him; In truth, his lot is wondrous well bested."

Like Jesus who told us that "the Kingdom of God is within you," Omar claims that one can attain mystic union with God in the "here and now." This is the universal insight repeated by all mystics throughout the ages. When our primary goal is to truly seek and love God, we are joined by persons from a diversity of religious affiliations, and academic arguments on textual minutia become irrelevant:

#49 In Synagogue and cloister, mosque and school, Hell's terrors and heaven's lures men's bosoms rule, But they who master Allah's mysteries, Sow not this empty chaff their heart to fool.

Omar explains that some time may be needed to achieve mystic unity with God—it can't be bought or obtained through reason alone:

#302 The "Truth" will not be shown to lofty thought, Nor yet with lavished gold may it be bought; But, if you yield your life for fifty years, From words to "states" you may perchance be brought.

One of the many points argued by scholars is Omar's meaning of the word, "wine." Obviously, wine is forbidden in Islam. Is the meaning of "wine" literal, symbolic, or both? Personally, I think Omar often uses "wine" literally as "beverage," but he also uses it metaphorically to express "mystical ecstasy." In this stanza, "wine" is clearly symbolic:

#262 In taverns better far commune with Thee Than pray in mosques and fail Thy face to see! Oh, first and last of all Thy creatures Thou 'Tis Thine to burn, and Thine to cherish me!

In this stanza, the meaning of "wine" is literal:

#349 Tell Khayyam, for a master of the schools, He strangely misinterprets my plain rules: Where have I said that wine is wrong for all? 'Tis lawful for the wise, but not for fools.

In all Abrahamic religions (Judaism, Christianity, and Islam), there is tension between GOOD WORKS and GRACE as the basis for Salvation. Is Heaven earned by good works or does God's unconditional love insure our place in Heaven? Another paradox involves EVIL: If God is all- powerful, why does evil endure:

#102 If grace be grace, and Allah gracious be, Adam from Paradise why banished He? Grace to poor sinners shown is grace indeed; In grace hard-earned by works no grace I see.

This verse speaks to the philosophy of the late Russian mystic Rasputin who saw sin as a prerequisite to redemption:

#46 Khayyam! Why weep you that your life is bad? What boots it thus to mourn? Rather be glad.

He that sins not can make no claim to mercy, Mercy was made for sinners – be not sad.

Omar touches on the idea of predestination, which is a major theological position in Islam, as well as the "Christianity" of Protestant Reformer John Calvin. As an astronomer, Omar is aware of the predictability of most of the visible cosmos, and he fears that predestination is a possibility:

#100 When Allah mixed my clay, He knew full well My future acts, and could each one foretell; Without His will no act of mine was wrought; Is it then just to punish me in Hell?

One of the recurring analogies in Omar's poetry is God as "potter" and humankind as "pots." Literally, we are made of dust, and to dust we return. Omar reminds us that the clay in our earthenware cup could, in the past, have been human:

#32 This jug did once like me, love's sorrows taste, And bonds of beauty's tresses once embraced.

This handle, when you see upon its side, Has many a time twined round a slender waist!

He acknowledges the possibility that there may be no afterlife:

#107 Drink wine! Long must you sleep within the tomb, Without a friend, or wife to cheer your gloom; Hear what I say, and tell it not again, "Never again can withered tulips bloom."

He hopes that, at death, all our questions will be answered:

#87 Make haste! Soon must you quit this life below, And pass the veil, and Allah's secrets know; Make haste to take your pleasure while you may, You wot not whence you come, nor whither go.

This stanza is a favorite of mine and Joseph Campbell's:

#491 Man is a cup, his soul the wine therein, Flesh is a pipe, spirit the voice within; O Khayyam, have you fathomed what man is? A magic lantern with a light therein!

Omar knows he is a heretic and cannot be otherwise:

#60 From Mosque an outcast, and to church a foe, Allah! Of what clay didst thou form me so? Like sceptic monk or ugly courtesan, No hopes have I above, no joys below.

Omar is comfortable with Christianity – in the sense that all religions are one:

#293 Did no fair rose my paradise adorn, I would make shift to deck it with a thorn; And if I lacked my prayer-mats, beads, and Shaikh, Those Christian bells and stoles I would not scorn.

A discussion about Omar wouldn't be complete without mentioning his affinity for Zoroastrians. Another Sufi, Attar of Nishapur, went so far as to declare, "We are the eternal Magians – we're not Moslems." Attar felt that the Islamic religion, as it was practiced, lacked the quality of love that dominated the old Persian religion of Zoroaster and Christianity. In the next verse, Omar talks about being a Zoroastrian and not being a good Moslem:

#281 Oft times I plead my foolishness to Thee, My heart contracted with perplexity; I gird me with the Magian zone, and why? For shame so poor a Moslem to be.

Some scholars postulate that Omar was a Zoroastrian and that his frequent use of "tavern" is a symbol for "Magian fire temple," but the following verse suggests otherwise:

#334 Am I a wine-bibber? What if I am? Zoroastrian or infidel? Suppose I am? Each sect miscalls me, but I heed them not, I am my own, and what I am, I am.

Sufiism is pantheist or panentheist. Pantheist means that God is all. Panentheist means that God is all and more. Panentheism is acceptable to Islam – as it is to Christianity, Judaism, and Zoroastrianism. The next verse speaks to this:

#389 Nor you nor I can read the eternal decree To that enigma we can find no key; They talk of you and me behind the veil But, if that veil be lifted, where are we?

The mystic knows the panentheistic reality that God is everywhere, although many people fail to realize this or take the time to recognize it. The following verse echoes William Blake's idea that, if the doors of perception were cleansed, all could see the reality of God and God's Universe:

#247 The world is baffled in its search for Thee, Wealth cannot find Thee, no, nor poverty; Thou'rt very near us, but our ears are deaf, Our eyes are blinded that we may not see!

Omar also expressed his belief that nothing bad can come from God – the same doctrine of Universal Salvation espoused by Zoroaster and Universalist Christians:

#305 Allah, our Lord, is merciful, though just; Sinner! Despair not, but His mercy trust! For though today you perish in your sins, Tomorrow He'll absolve your crumbling dust.

#318 Sure of thy grace, for sins why need I fear? How can the pilgrim faint whilst Thou art near? On the last day Thy grace will wash me white, And all my "black record" will disappear.

#193 They say, when the last trump shall sound its knell, Our Friend will sternly judge, and doom to hell.

Can aught but good from perfect goodness come? Compose your trembling hearts, 'twill all be well.

#276 O Thou! Who know'st the secret thoughts of all, In time of sorest need who aidest all, Grant me repentance, and accept my plea, O Thou who dost accept the pleas of all!

#204 Can alien Pharisees Thy kindness tell, Like us, Thy intimates, who nigh Thee dwell? Thou say'st, "All sinners will I burn with fire." Say that to strangers, we know Thee too well!

This last verse refers to mystical insight in which the knowledge of God is gained directly. Like mystics and Universalists everywhere, Omar knows that in the end, we will ALL be united with God.

CHAPTER 14

Universal Salvation in Hinduism and its Children

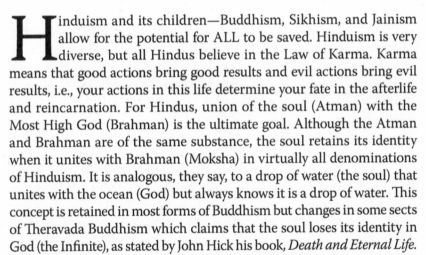

Hinduism and its children—Buddhism, Sikhism, and Jainism allow for the potential for ALL to be saved. Hinduism is very diverse, but all Hindus believe in the Law of Karma. Karma means that good actions bring good results and evil actions bring evil results, i.e., your actions in this life determine your fate in the afterlife and reincarnation. For Hindus, union of the soul (Atman) with the Most High God (Brahman) is the ultimate goal. Although the Atman and Brahman are of the same substance, the soul retains its identity when it unites with Brahman (Moksha) in virtually all denominations of Hinduism. It is analogous, they say, to a drop of water (the soul) that unites with the ocean (God) but always knows it is a drop of water. This concept is retained in most forms of Buddhism but changes in some sects of Theravada Buddhism which claims that the soul loses its identity in God (the Infinite), as stated by John Hick his book, *Death and Eternal Life*.

In Hinduism, the high God (Brahman) is beyond form, but is manifest in many forms (gods).

After all, how is God manifest to a hamster? Here are some Hindu verses that speak to this:

"Whatever form any devotee with faith wishes to worship Me, I make that faith of his steady" (Bhagavad-Gita 7.21).

"Whosoever offers to Me with devotion a leaf, a flower, a fruit, or water- that offering of Love, of the pure-hearted I accept" (Bhagavad-Gita 9.29).

"By Me is pervaded all this universe, by Me in the form of the unmanifest.

All beings rest in Me, and I do not rest in them" (Bhagavad-Gita 9.4).

Buddhism does not does not deal with God per se, but rather is a "fast track" salvation system of the reincarnation type which allows for the Buddhist to attach him/herself to other religions such as the shamanic Bon religion of Tibet, Daoism in China, or the Shinto religion in Japan.

Most Westerners think that reincarnation is instantaneous, but this is not generally so. For the overwhelming majority of Hindus and Buddhists, there is an intermediate state between death and rebirth. This intermediate state is presided over by Yama or Yamaraj. In Hindu mythology, Yama was the first king and king of the dead. His assistants weigh your good deeds and bad deeds and, depending on the outcome, send you to Heaven or Hell for three generations. Other Hindus assert that Karma is constantly reassessed on a sort of "Karma credit card," and that the length of your stay in Heaven or Hell is determined by how much "good" or "bad Karma you have "charged." Obviously your Karma also determines your fate regarding reincarnation. Saviors (avatars) are also a part of Hinduism. Dying with the name of Vishnu or one of his incarnations on your lips (such as Rama or Krishna), assures that all of your sins will be taken away and you advance directly to paradise. The last words of Gandhi were, "Rama, Rama."

In Buddhism, as in its parent religion, Yama judges the dead. Yama is known as "Yama" in Tibet, Nepal, Southeast Asia and Western China. In Eastern China, Korea, and Japan, his name changes, but he is always the same fair judge of the dead. Although he is the king of Heaven in Hinduism, he presides over Hell in Buddhism. In the *Tibetan Book of the Dead*, a twelfth century Buddhist work, the intermediate state before rebirth lasts 49 days, before you are reincarnated.

In Pure Land Buddhism, by invoking the name of the "savior" Bodhisattva Amitabha Buddha at death, you will be transported to a Pure Land of Bliss by Amitabha (the Buddha of Infinite Light), who is also known as O-Mi-To (China) and Amida (Japan). Once there, you can continue the process of liberation under blissful conditions for as long as it takes. Other Pure Land Savior Bodhisattvas include Ti-tsang and Guanyin (Khuan-Yin) the female Bodhisattva of Compassion.

The other children of Hinduism, Sikhism and Jainism, also have a judgment after death by Yama (king of the Dead), reincarnation, and the potential for ALL to achieve union with God (the Infinite).

Sikhism is a merger of Islam and Hinduism that developed in the sixteenth century when its founder, Guru Narnak, had a revelation from God. The god of the Sikhs is a personal god, much like the god of the Abrahamic religions; however, the Sikh salvation system is the Hindu model of reincarnation in which ALL have the potential to reach the highest state. "How then is truth to be attained? How is the veil of illusion to be destroyed? Narnak says, 'through obedience to the divine order, which is written in your heart.'"

Jainism is a religion of the "axial age" (sixth century BCE), when Mahavira, the last of its twenty-four "holy ones," appeared. Hindus and religious scholars see Jainism as an off-shoot of Hinduism, but some Jains maintain that it evolved independently. Jains see the Universe as having always existed, but having different eons or ages. Humans reincarnate through heavens, earth, and hells, but ALL have the possibility of reaching the infinite.

So we see that Universalism is fundamental to the ancient religion of Hinduism and its children. Hell is not permanent in the intermediate state between death and rebirth, and the process of reincarnation allows for ALL to ultimately unite with God (the Infinite). Some years ago, I was attending a Hindu workshop for teachers, and they talked about their religious "children," namely, Buddhism, Sikhism, and Jainism. I can't recall if there was a Jain in attendance, but I do remember talking at length with the Sikh who presented that day. Can you imagine this happening with Western religions? Think of a Zoroastrian conference where Jews, Christians and Moslems show up and congenially admit that Zoroastrianism is the basis for all three of their religions!

CHAPTER 15

Scientific Investigation of the "Dark Side"

Religious experiences, currently known by the term, "Spiritually Transformative Experiences" (STEs) have been studied scientifically for the past 150 years by social scientists and biomedical researchers. For purposes of this study, Spiritually Transformative Experiences have been divided into four categories:

1. Religious/Spiritual/Mystical Experiences (RSMEs),
2. Near-Death Experiences (NDEs),
3. Death-Bed Visions (DBVs), and
4. After-Death Communications (ADCs).

While most reported STEs are "positive" in that they are pleasant and provide clarity or insight, a significant minority of reported cases are "negative" in that they are frightening. As indicated by the word, "Transformative," the most consistent characteristic of both positive and negative STEs is that they CHANGE PEOPLE'S LIVES.

Most of you know me as a Professor of Psychology, but you may not realize that my main research focus over the past 30 years has been to ascertain the role that religious experience plays in the human psyche. The material I research can usually be found in no more than one or two chapters of a Psychology of Religion textbook. Just let me remind you again: Research into Spiritual Experiences CAN BE and IS conducted using the same criteria that we use to investigate any other psychological phenomena (Vincent, 2006). These include:

1. Case studies of transpersonal experience,
2. Sociological surveys that tell who and what percentage of the population have STEs,
3. Psychological tests that measure not only the mental health of the individual but also evaluate the depth of mystical experiences,
4. Biomedical and neuroscience testing, including the EEG, PET-scan, and functional MRI to, in some cases, document genuine altered states of consciousness and demonstrate that mystical experiences are not just wishful thinking; additionally EEGs and EKGs allow us to document death in NDEs that occur in hospitals,
5. Sociological and psychological investigations that assess the after-effects these experiences have on people, and
6. Controlled experimental research (such as Panke's experiment testing psychedelics) (Smith, 2000, pp. 99-105).

Even though we are talking about human experience that is basically "religious" in nature, scientists have a legitimate role to investigate it using all the tools of analysis at our disposal. In this way, we separate ourselves from the sensational and fictitious accounts of the *National Enquirer* and gradually move toward a greater understanding of the broad spectrum of human experience.

Surveys of Spiritually Transformative Experiences

Current research documents the following facts:

1. A large percentage of the population have experienced STEs,
2. The overwhelming majority of those having STEs are mentally normal and not psychotic, and
3. STEs change people's lives for the better (Vincent, 2006).

To date, research has shown that negative STEs are far less common than positive ones. In his initial study of 3,000 cases of STEs sent to the Religious Experience Research Centre (RERC) (formerly at Oxford; now at University of Wales Lampeter), Sir Alister Hardy (1979, p.28) found 4% negative. Somewhat later, using 4,000 cases at the RERC, Merete Jakobsen (1999, p. iv) also found 4% negative experiences. Recently, Zinzhong Yao and Paul Badham (2007, pp. 9,45-46) of the RERC found in studying 3,196 Chinese that 56.7% had religious experiences, but only 8.5% of them were negative. They compared this to a 1987 British survey which found 12% negative experiences (Yao & Badham 2007, p. 185). Regarding NDEs, in a monumental analysis of over 21 studies, Nancy Evans Bush (2006) found 17.2% of them to be negative. Also, most researchers of STEs feel that the numbers are under-reported because of the stigma sometimes associated with having a negative STE.

Judgment and Afterlife in Ancient and Modern World Religions

Do Spiritually Transformative Experiences prove the existence of a God who interacts with us personally? Do encounters with dead humans prove the existence of an afterlife? From my perspective, they point in that direction for this reason: Virtually all religions have their genesis in the Spiritually Transformative Experience of their founder. Also, the subsequent theology of virtually all ancient and contemporary religions includes some form of Judgment by Divine Beings and subsequent relegation to Heaven or Hell based on the ratio of good to bad deeds of the deceased person while on Earth. Hell, of course, is the ultimate experience of the "Dark Side." Before we go any further, it is important to realize that when one studies the experiential aspect of comparative religion that THE ANGELS, SAINTS, AND JINN OF THE WEST = THE SMALL "g" GODS OF THE EAST AND OF ANCIENT TIMES because they perform the same function. This will become apparent as we look at some variations in cultural expectations surrounding Judgment.

In Ancient Egypt, we have a Judgment in the *Book of the Dead* whereby the heart of the deceased is weighed against a feather, and woe to those whose heart is heavy with sin! This Judgment is presided over by the savior god Osiris and his wife Isis (Budge, 1895/1967, pp. 253-261).

Later, in Zoroastrianism (the religion of the Magi), Judgment is conducted by three angels whose duty is to weigh the good deeds against the bad deeds of the deceased. If his or her life reflects an overwhelming preponderance of GOOD deeds, they are allowed to proceed across a WIDE bridge; if the deceased has been more evil than good, the bridge becomes narrow, and he or she falls into hell. This same bridge imagery lives on in Shiite Islam where it is the job of the Angel Gabriel to hold the divine scales of Judgment (Vincent, 1999, pp.5-6; Masumian, 1995, p.79).

In Judaism, according to the *Book of Daniel* (12:1-3), the Archangel Michael holds the scales of Judgment on which the deeds of the deceased are weighed. In Medieval Christian artwork, the Archangel Michael still holds the scales, but Jesus sits above him as judge.

Now let us move from West to East. In Hinduism and its children, Buddhism, Sikhism, and Jainism, Yamaraj (King Yama) is the judge of the dead. In all these religions, weighing your good deeds against your bad deeds on the divine scales of justice determines not only whether or not you go to heaven or hell in the intermediate state but also the status of your next life after reincarnation (Masumian, 1995, pp.5-7, 143). To me, reincarnation is the only major theological difference in world religions. The East has it, and in the West, reincarnation is only a minority position (such as in the Christianity of the Gnostics and the Islamic sect of the Druze). We see these same themes repeated in the Native American religions of North America, Mezzo-America, and South America where the themes of Paradise and Punishment are repeated (Nigosian, 2000, pp. 382, 384). In virtually all religions, assignment of the deceased to the "Dark Side" is either 1) determined by God's emissaries or 2) determined by the natural law of the universe.

Near-Death Experiences

Now let us look at the "Dark Side" of the NDE. In an article in *Psychiatry* journal, Bruce Greyson and Nancy Evans Bush (1992) identified three types of negative NDEs.

1. The first type is the NDE that is initially frightening but later turns positive, most often after the person calls out to God or God's emissary.
2. The second type is a non-existent or "eternal void" experience— in other words, an existential hell.
3. The third type is a "graphic and hellish landscape and entities."

In her book *Blessing in Disguise*, Dr. Barbara Rommer (2000, p. 87-96) adds a fourth category of a frightening life-review.

The following two examples describe distressing near-death experiences that turn positive. (Note that both contain graphic imagery of hell.)

"I was in hell ... I cried up to God, and it was by the power of God and the mercy of God that I was permitted to come back." (Rommer, 2000, p. 42)

"God, I'm not ready, please help me ... I remember when I screamed (this), an arm shot out of the sky and grabbed my hand at the last second. I was falling off the end of the funnel, the lights flashing; and the heat was really something." (Greyson & Bush, 1992, p. 100)

Next is an example of both the void and a frightening life review:

"It was not peaceful, much baggage, much unfinished business. All things are connected. You are not your body, you are a soul. Mine was in limbo. I knew I would be in limbo for a long time. I had a life review and was sent to the void. The life review was so disquieting. I saw many different ways my life could have taken. I saw my past life in there and other past lives I was unable to recall. (Vincent, 1994, p. 119)

It is interesting to note that these experiences are highly similar despite differences in time or culture. Thomas Harriot (who was a member of the Jamestown Colony in seventeenth century Virginia) recorded two stories of NDEs told to him by the Roanoke Indians which, significantly, took place prior to the arrival of the British settlers. The first story told of an Indian who died and was buried; the next day, the grave seemed to move, and he was dug up. He told of being very near a terrible place of torment, but the gods saved him and let him come back to life to teach his friends what they should do to avoid hell. The second story was similar, except that in this story, the Indian went to Paradise (Baym, pp. 76 - 80).

James McClenon (1991) discusses NDEs in Medieval China and Japan. In one case, he tells of a ruler named Muh who died but revived two and a half days later. He told of meeting the Emperor of Heaven, hearing beautiful music, seeing 10,000 dances, and returning to life with prophetic information. Prof. McClenon notes that these Medieval Taoist NDEs resemble modern ones.

Deathbed Visions

The next example describes the DBV of a seventh century Mahayana (Northern) Buddhist. They believe that the Amida Buddha is a "savior god" who can rescue you from hell and take you to the pure land of bliss. Once there, you can work out your final ascent to Nirvana under blissful conditions. "A butcher is dying. He first has a vision of hell, whereupon he was terrified into chanting the name of 'Amida;' He then had a vision of the Amida Buddha offering him a lotus seat and passed peacefully away." (McClenon, 1994, p.176)

After-Death Communications

If a negative ADC is delivered by a STRANGER, he or she is properly termed a "ghost!" If it comes from some super-human entity, it is usually called a "demon." The following two examples are taken from Merete Jakobsen's *Negative Spiritual Experiences: Encounters with Evil* (pp.17, 21). The first is an evil presence in a British house;

> "This evil presence was masculine and seemed to come from the wall facing me, nearer and nearer as though straining to get me. I saw nothing but the blackness of the room, as my sister had (previously), but although it is 20 years or more ago, I'll never disbelieve that there are powers of evil. A very violent family had lived there."

The second account is Danish and takes place in the woods.

> "As we progressed, I found several dead birds along the path. We reached an open space where there had been a bonfire. I felt more and more anxious and eventually said to my husband, 'I don't know how you feel, but I have a sense of evil and horror in this wood.' My husband said he had not wanted to tell me, but he had heard that a satanic cult had used the wood. I wanted to go home immediately. I find it extraordinary that human evil can change the whole atmosphere in a large wood."

Religious/Spiritual/Mystical Experiences.

There are ancient and modern accounts of tours of the afterlife. St. Paul, in II Cor. 12 tells us of his out-of-body experience in which he is transported to the third level of heaven. Mohammed in Sura 17:1 of the Quran, tells us of his out-of-body experience in which he also is transported to heaven. Other religious figures in history have had encounters with evil, including Jesus' encounter with Satan recorded in the Synoptic Gospels and Buddha's encounter with the demon, Mara. The following is St. Teresa of Availa's account of her mystical experience of hell:

"The entrance, I thought, resembled a very long, narrow passage like a furnace, very low, dark and closely confined; the ground seemed to be full of water which looked like filthy, evil-smelling mud, and in it were many wicked-looking reptiles. At the end, there was a hollow place scooped out of a wall like a cupboard, and it was there that I found myself in close confinement. But the sight of all this was pleasant by comparison to what I felt there ... I felt a fire within my soul, the nature of which I am utterly incapable of describing ... The fact is that I cannot find words to describe that interior fire and that despair which is greater than the most grievous torture and pains ... There was no light, and everything was in the blackest darkness" (Bush, 2002).

There are accounts of individuals who are given tours of both heaven and hell. One is the story of Arda Viraf, a nineth century follower of the religion of the Magi who was given hensbane (a non-hallucinogenic drug) that put him in a coma for several days. (Segal, 2004, pp.195-196) The Magi had chosen him for this holy quest because of his righteousness. He awoke to tell of his tour of heaven and hell.

The psychiatrist George Richie (1998, pp.37-41) who had an NDE in 1943 tells of visiting hellish realms invisible but on the earth-plane, as well as tours of other realms where people were trapped because of their own desires. All around these lost souls were Beings of Light just waiting to assist them out of their hellish state. During his NDE, Richie reports that he was given this tour by Jesus Christ himself! Regarding mystical religious experiences, Merete Jakobsen (1999, p.52) notes that evil encounters are terminated when the person calls upon God or God's emissary, usually through prayer or religious rituals.

Hell is for Rehabilitation and Is Not Eternal

Is there a way out of hell? Most (but not all) religious experience researchers think so. Both Nancy Evans Bush (2002) and Barbara Rommer (2000, p. 27) note that these negative NDEs are for instruction and are thought to be a "wake-up call" to those who have them. This echoes the purpose of hellish experience as expressed in the *Tibetan Book of the Dead* (Evans-Wentz, pp. 28-68). Both the Northern Buddhist and Universalist Christian traditions have saviors (Amida Buddha and Jesus) who rescue people from hell (Vincent, 2005, p. 8).

In the New Testament book of I Peter (3:18-20; 4:6, NRSV), it is stated that Jesus descended into hell after his crucifixion but before his resurrection: "For Christ also suffered for sins once and for all, the righteous for the unrighteous in order to bring you to God. He was put to death in the flesh, but made alive in the spirit in which also he went and made a proclamation to the spirits in prison, who in former times did not obey." "For this reason, the gospel was proclaimed even to the dead, so that though they had been judged in the flesh as everyone is, they might live in the spirit as God does."

It would seem from modern NDE accounts like some of those mentioned above; Jesus is still rescuing people from hell (Vincent, 2003). There is also an interesting eighteenth century autobiographical NDE account by Dr. George deBenneville who died of a "consumption-like" illness and revived at his wake 42 hours later (Vincent & Morgan, 2006). He told of seeing angels rescuing people from hell, after they had repented.

As in the Buddhist DBV above, the Amida Buddha stands ready to save any human who finds him or herself in hell if they call out to him as few as ten times (Nigosian, 2000, p.89). It should be noted that in all of the Eastern religions, hell is not permanent but is a method for instruction. In the West, this was the view of the Christian church for its first 500 years but has become a minority view since that time (Hanson, 1899/2007, p. 139-141). In Islam, there are a few references in the Hadith to the view that hell is not permanent, but this view is held by only a few of the Sufis (Vincent, 2005, p. 12).

Conclusion

Only 150 years ago, scientific research into STEs began. The scientific methods used to do this research are the same as those used to research any other social or biomedical phenomena. We now know that, like positive STEs, negative STEs are widespread, that they occur in people who are normal and not mentally ill, and that they change people's lives for the better. While it may be too early to reach any final theological conclusions from this data, it would appear that there is a universal underpinning to the religions of the world, that humans are accountable for their actions, and that nothing good is ever lost.

CHAPTER 16

Magic, Deeds, and Universalism

~

W hen I was a freshman at Baylor University, I took a required religion class from Prof. Kyle Yates. Professor Yates was one of the scholars who worked on the Revised Standard Version of the Old Testament (a.k.a. the Hebrew Bible). When we got to the Persian period of Hebrew history, he began to talk about Zoroaster, the prophet of the Magi. Inspired by his lectures, I went to the library and read the hymns of Zoroaster and thought to myself, "Wow! God talked to someone who wasn't Jewish!" This started my life-long quest for the generic God in the world's religions.

For many years, I've been active in interfaith work, and my friends and colleagues here in Houston form a tapestry of the world's religions. I have learned from them. Now that I'm retired, I'm a little old man who "lives" on the fourth floor of the Rice University Library, still steeped in the world's religions.

Today, I will be your guide to the Afterlife. You may have been hoping for Beatrice and Dante, but the editor wasn't quite able to conjure them up. I'm going to give you a three-layer view of how people—both ancient and modern—have viewed Afterlife. This is what we in psychology call a "developmental" view of religion because it reflects the way both individuals and societies normally mature.

The most rudimentary level of religious development is Magic, which includes bribery or other manipulation of the gods in order to guarantee a positive outcome for your Afterlife. In the middle layer, Afterlife is dependent on your Deeds during your life on Earth, and the history of religious art illustrates the development of this idea across time and cultures. (Interestingly, Magic has often been practiced in conjunction with Deeds.) The top layer of development is Universalism, the concept that God is too good to condemn anyone to Eternal Hell, and that all humans will go to Heaven, either immediately or eventually.

One important thing to know about the study of comparative religion is that it is a wide-open field with many scholars from various disciplines participating, such as Joseph Campbell (literature), Mircea Eliade (history), Paul Brunton (philosophy), Karl Jung (psychiatry), and Sir James Frazier (anthropology). Today, we'll touch on the Afterlife from the perspectives of religion, history, psychology, sociology, and art. Most people in the world, regardless of their religion, believe that judgment for the Afterlife is determined by one's deeds in this life. Simply stated, if your good deeds outweigh your bad deeds, you go to Heaven. But if your bad deeds outweigh your good deeds, you go to Hell. This is the story of humanity. My point is that human beings across time and culture share one story, although I must tell you that in the East, after an intermediate stage of Heaven or Hell, you have a "sequel"—called "reincarnation." In other words, in the East, your deeds affect not only your intermediate destination of Heaven or Hell, but also determine the condition of your next life.

Deeds

The oldest judgment scene we have in art is a depiction of the *Egyptian Book of the Dead* which has been seen in tomb art as early as about 3,000 BCE. After the deceased goes into the darkness (which is the body of Nut), he or she comes forth into the light, into the Great Hall of Truth. Osiris is the King of the Afterlife, and Isis is his queen. For over 3,500 years, Osiris was known as the "Resurrection and the Life." Your deeds in life were judged by weighing your heart against a feather, and woe to those whose heart is heavy with sin!

Next we have judgment in Zoroastrianism, the religion of the Magi. Here, three angels preside over judgment—Mithra, Sarosha, and Rashnu. Rashnu holds the scales, Sarosha is the judge, and Mithra listens to appeals. Your good deeds are weighed against your bad deeds, and then you pass over a bridge. If your good deeds are heavier, the bridge is wide open to you, and you pass over easily. If your evil deeds outweigh your good ones, the bridge becomes narrow, and you fall into Hell. This razor-sharp bridge imagery lives on in Shi'ite Islam.

In the Hebrew Bible, in the Book of Daniel (12:1-3), it is the Archangel Michael who presides over the resurrection. Judaism for the most part forbids artwork, but in Christianity, Michael takes his place right below Jesus in the judgment of the dead. It is Michael who holds the scales in which your deeds are weighed. This same scene is repeated in Islam, but here the Archangel holding the scales is Gabriel.

Next we move from West to East. Most Westerners think that reincarnation is instantaneous, but this is not generally so. For the overwhelming majority of Hindus and Buddhists, there is an intermediate state between death and re-birth. This intermediate state is presided over by Yama or Yamaraj. In Hindu mythology, Yama was the first king and king of the dead. His assistants weigh your good deeds and, depending on the outcome, you go to Heaven or Hell for three generations. In Buddhism, as in its parent religion, Yama judges the dead. Yama is known as "Yama" in Tibet, Nepal, Southeast Asia and Western China. In Eastern China, Korea, and Japan, his name changes, but he is always the same fair judge of the dead. Where he is the King of Heaven in Hinduism, he presides over Hell in Buddhism. In the *Tibetan Book of the Dead,* a twelfth-century Buddhist work, the intermediate state lasts for 49 days before you are re-born.

Magic

Now let's step back to analyze the way magic is used to influence Afterlife. Obviously, we are aware of cultures in both the Eastern and Western hemispheres that have used human or animal sacrifice to bribe the gods to do or not do something the petitioner asks. However, this practice has been abandoned by the world's major religions and can be found in only indigenous religions today. On the other hand, belief in magical powers is still very much a part of our modern culture when it comes to "stacking the deck" in favor of a Heavenly Afterlife. In most religion, there is a tension between the moral justice of judgment according to deeds and magic to insure a positive verdict.

The keys to effective magic are that, 1) you have to be "in the club", and 2) you or your priest must know the "secret words." In ancient Egypt, the scales of judgment are older than the pyramids, but they co-exist with the magic text of the *Egyptian Book of the Dead* that enables the deceased to overcome past sins. Countering this are not only the scales, but the instruction for Merikare (2200 BCE) which reinforces the idea of judgment according to deeds.

Additionally, there is the story of Si-Osiris (son of Osiris) and his father, Setne Khaemwise (fourth son of Ramesses II). Si-Osiris is a seer. He and his father watched a funeral procession in which a rich man was being carried with his elaborate belongings to a princely tomb. Shortly after this, they observed the funeral of a poor man wrapped only in a cloth who was being taken for burial in the desert sand. The Egyptian prince remarks to his son that he hopes for a good funeral in preparation for a glorious Afterlife, but his seer son remarks that all things are not as they appear to be. He puts his father into a trance, and the two are transported to the land of the dead where the evil rich man is suffering a hellish fate and the righteous poor man is being comforted by Osiris, Isis, and the Egyptian gods, and is living afterlife in regal splendor. This shows the development of morality and justice in the Egyptian religion, and some Christian scholars think this is the origin of the story of the rich man and Lazarus in the Gospel of Luke (Lk 16:19-31). The main point here is to underscore the great antiquity of the belief that salvation is by works.

In ancient Greece, the Afterlife in very early times was seen as a very gloomy place where everyone went. But by the time of Plato, the idea of judgment according to deeds had developed. In Plato's *Republic*, the story is told about Er, the world's earliest recorded near-death experiencer, who revives on his funeral pyre and tells of a judgment at death by three judges. The good ascend to Paradise, and the evil descend to Hell. But after a period of time, Plato also mentions reincarnation. Pythagoras also was an advocate of reincarnation.

In the mysteries that were popular in the later Greek and Roman periods, we are given a chance for an "up-grade" in the Afterlife via the magical rites of the mysteries of Orpheus, Dionysus, Demeter and Persephone, Mithra, Isis and Osiris, etc. According to the mysteries of Orpheus, one of the things you were to say was, "I am a child of Earth and the starry Heaven, but Heaven is my home." Here again, you have to be in the club, and you have to know the secret words.

In ancient Judaism, the sins of the Jewish people were magically put into a goat (scapegoat) on the Day of Atonement. Here again, you have to be "in the club" and you (or the priest) have to know the secret words (Lev. 16:21-22). Modern Jews no longer do this, knowing that God hears our prayers. Judaism in its early years presented a shadowy Afterlife called Sheol which was very similar to the Hades of early Greece. Jewish writing from 400 – 100 BCE which is found in the Catholic, Orthodox, Eastern Orthodox, and Coptic Christian Bibles (which Protestants refer to as the Apocrypha) have some references to a Heaven or Hell state prior to the last judgment (II Esdras 7:75-101). The Apocryphal books also abound with angels who are named (e.g.Raphael in the Book of Tobit). The Jewish Pseudepigrapha (200 BCE – 70 CE) have Heaven and Hell (especially Enoch I, II, and III). These books of Enoch are not in the Hebrew Bible, and only first Enoch made it into the Coptic Christian Bible. The books were, however used by the Essenes and figure into the Judaism prior to the destruction of the Temple in 70 CE. The Rule of Community (also known as the Manual of Discipline) and the War of the Sons of Light and the Sons of Darkness in the Dead Sea Scrolls of the Essenes are especially rich in imagery of Heaven and Hell. After 70 CE, Rabbinic Judaism developed, and the resulting Hebrew Bible has references to Sheol, the Messianic Time and to the Last Judgment in the Book of Daniel.

In Christianity, this magic level is practiced by those who say that "belief in Jesus" assures an exclusive ticket to Heaven. You have to be "in the club" (that is, be a Christian), and you have to know the secret words, which in Fundamentalist Christianity are found in John 3:16 or John 14:6. While Liberal Christians and many moderate Christians see Jesus as the "suffering servant" of Isaiah who died to bring us the word, Fundamentalist Christians delight in being "saved."

That belief alone will save you is an idea as old as the followers of the Hindu gods Shiva and Lord Krishna. Its positive side is the devotional path in which the followers identify with and emulate the god. In Christianity, we see this positive emulation in those kind and loving souls who model their lives on Jesus. One is reminded of the words of the beautiful old Gospel hymn, "In the Garden": "He walks with me, and He talks with me, and He tells me I am His own." In Hinduism, the devotional path is expressed in the prayer, "Krishna, Krishna, Hare, Hare", in other words, "Krishna, Krishna, Redeemer, Redeemer." Magic in Hinduism is best illustrated by the idea that if you die with the name of Vishnu or one of his incarnations, such as Rama or Krishna, on your lips all of your sins are taken away and you go straight to Nirvana (heaven). There are times when we all need a little magic. The last words of Gandhi were Rama, Rama.

In Buddhism, magic is represented in the *Tibetan Book of the Dead*. Being "in the club" (that is, being Buddhist) and having your relative or a monk read the secret words of the Book of the Dead by your corpse. This will enable you to become aware in the Afterlife and chose the things which will assure you a good re-birth. Also in Pure Land Buddhism by invoking the name of the Amitabha (the Buddha of Infinite Light), at death, you will be transported to a Pure Land of Bliss in the West. Amitabha is known as O-Mi-To (China) and Amida (Japan). (Flotz, 2004, p. 73; Nigosian, 2000, p. 89). There you can continue the process of liberation under blissful conditions. Other "savior" Bodhisattvas are Ti-tsang and Guanyin and anyone who chants their name will have their sins wiped away (Teiser, 1988, p. 187).

Universalism

Having looked at the developmental level below judgment by deeds, let us look at the level above it:

Universalism. The concept of Universalism as an idea is as old as Zoroaster. Around 1600 – 1200 BCE (like Moses, the exact date of his life is not know), Zoroaster preached these basic concepts; see if they sound familiar: "God - Satan, Good - Evil, Light - Darkness, Angels - Demons, Death - Judgment, Heaven - Hell, and at the end of time, Resurrection of the Body and Life Everlasting." He also preached that, "There is a long period of punishment for the wicked and reward for the pious, but thereafter, eternal joy shall reign forever" (Yasna 30.11). In other words, Hell is for rehabilitation, not for torture. This idea may be as old as Zoroaster, but it is as new as modern-day near-death experiencers, many of whom died into Hell but found themselves rescued when they called out to God or (in the West) called out to God or Jesus.

In Judaism, Universalism is reflected in the Messianic Time described primarily in the Book of Isaiah (Is 2:2 & 4, 12:1-2, 25:6-8, 39:3, 5, 66:18 & 23, Jer 31:31-34). The Rabbis of the Midrash say that one can stay in Hell only one year.

In Christianity, the idea of Universalism is a very old and enduring theological position. Its major proponent in early Christianity was Origen (185 – 254 CE). In the nineteenth century, the Universalist Church was for a time the fifth or sixth largest denomination in the United States. In the twenty-first century, Universalism is advocated by

Christians from diverse backgrounds, including some post-Vatican II Catholics and Primitive Baptists. The Biblical references which support Universal Salvation are second in number only to Good Works as the way to Salvation. Other religions have Universalist hopes too. Although not in the Koran, it is written in the Hadith (the oral history of Mohammad) that, "Surely a day will come over Hell when there shall not be a human soul in it." The Bahai religion sees a continuous progression of souls toward perfection after death. In the East, Hinduism and its children— Buddhism, Sikhism, and Jainism—all allow for the potential for all to be saved. When Pam and I attended the Jade Buddha Temple a few years ago, they were singing, "We are not discouraged by the time it takes to save all the humans and all of the animals."

When one looks at the plight of humanity through the eyes of a parent, it is easy to see that Universalism makes sense. God is infinitely nicer than the best human beings you know. If you are a panentheist like me, you know that God is in all of us, and we are all in God. God knows the assets and limitations of each human soul. Unlike the State Board of Pardons and Parole, God knows how to rehabilitate people. Once upon a time before time mattered, people worshiped the Great Spirit, saw every living thing as possessing a spirit, and saw Afterlife as a Happy Hunting Ground. That sounds Universalist to me. So maybe we have come full circle. To quote Jesus in the non-canonical Gospel of Thomas, "Have you discovered the beginning, then, so that you are seeking the end? For where the beginning is, the end will be." As a Universalist Christian, I look forward to the time when, as Jesus taught, God will save the Lost Sheep and the Prodigal Son.

CHAPTER 17

What the Near-Death Experience and Other Spiritually Transformative Experiences Teach Us About God and Afterlife

~

In 1975, the near-death experience burst into contemporary consciousness with the publication of Raymond Moody's famous book *Life After Life*. The public was newly fascinated, unaware that the phenomena had been described throughout recorded history (the story of Er in Plato's *Republic* being the most famous example).

Defining the NDE

In 1979, Sir Alister Hardy began his exploration all types of religious/spiritual/mystical experiences with the publication of his book *The Spiritual Nature of Man* in which he reported that one "trigger" for these phenomena was the "prospect of death." Working with cases from Hardy's original sample, Mark Fox in his book *Religion, Spirituality, and the Near-Death Experience* labeled these "crisis experiences" because it was unclear whether some persons had been clinically dead.

Some researchers include individuals who had come "close to death" in addition to those who were resuscitated after being clinically dead for a brief period of time. In their effort to clarify the terminology, Peter and Elizabeth Fenwick in their book *The Art of Dying* coined the term "temporary death experience" to separate those who came near to death from those who revived following clinical death.

Continuing this effort to define the characteristics of the NDE, Vince Migliore used a large sample from the files of the International Association of Near-Death Studies (IANDS) and published it in his book A *Measure of Heaven*. Comparing a sample of 193 accounts who had experienced clinical death to a sample of 189 accounts of "NDE-like" experiences (e.g., mystical experiences) who were not near death, Migliore found that the NDEs were more in-depth than the mystical experiences, but the difference was not statistically significant.

NDE Commonalities

People can and do have mystical experiences that resemble near-death experiences without dying. St. Paul's out-of-body experience (OBE) in which he went to heaven is a famous example (II Cor. 12). The NDE is unique among religious/mystical/spiritual experiences in that its "trigger" is clinical death, and we now have over 35 years of research that enable fascinating insights into what the NDE teaches us about God and afterlife. I begin with Jeff Long's "proofs of afterlife" from his book *Evidence of Afterlife* because of the magnitude of the sample (N=1300) and the fact that 613 subjects were given an objective questionnaire. They are as follows:

1. NDErs report increased alertness and consciousness
2. NDErs provide evidence from verifiable experiences OBEs
3. NDErs blind from birth report a form of "vision" during their NDE
4. NDErs report experiences while under anesthesia
5. NDErs report life reviews that include experiencing the feelings of others
6. NDErs report seeing dead relatives, including people unknown to them who were identified to them later by viewing family photographs

7. NDErs who are children report having every NDE element of older NDErs, and this is true whether their account is told during childhood or from an adult who had the experience in childhood

8. NDErs who were non-English-speakers from Jody and Jeff Long's database form the largest collection of cross-cultural NDEs and provide evidence that NDEs are the same all over the world

9. NDErs report that their lives were changed as a result of their NDE and, for the majority, the change was for the better.

To this list of "proofs," we can add the "Shared Death Experience" which Raymond Moody describes in his book *Glimpses of Eternity*. This occurs when a person or persons at the bedside of an individual who is dying experiences the beginning of the dying individual's first moments of death, including such things as alternate reality, mystical light, OBE, co-living the life review, unworldly or heavenly realms, and mist at death.

Basis for World Religions

Over a century ago, William James in *Varieties of Religious Experience* made the case that, "The founders of every church owed their power originally to the fact of their direct personal communication with the Divine." His research was reinforced by the work of Evelyn Underhill who in *Practical Mysticism* proclaimed, "This unmistakable experience has been achieved by the mystics of every religion; and when we read their statements, we know they are all speaking of the same thing." To me, the greatest contribution of Sir Alister Hardy and the Religious Experience Research Centre (RERC) has been to demonstrate that religious/spiritual/mystic experiences are, in fact, quite common. In *Conceptions of Afterlife in Early Civilizations*, Gregory Shushan makes the case that the NDE is the basis for afterlife accounts in the world's religions. His main points are:

1. There is a remarkable consistency among largely unconnected cultures and times regarding belief in life after death,

2. The core elements of these religious beliefs are largely similar to the core elements of the NDE,

3. These consistent beliefs in life after death contrast with the widely divergent creation myths of different religions.

In other words, the above studies (Long, Moody, Shushan) taken together demonstrate the NDE to be a world-wide phenomena and that it is at the generic core of afterlife beliefs in the world's religions. Organized religion is, at best, second-hand.

Insights into God and Afterlife

Using the same tools that social scientists employ to study all other facets of human behavior, researchers have gained fresh insights into how humans experience God in the here-and-now and in the hereafter. The following nine findings are the ones I personally find most compelling:

1. God (aka, Ultimate Reality/Great Spirit) is with us and not distant. Sir Alister Hardy in *The Spiritual Nature of Man* states that, from the evidence, God is "partly transcendent, and felt as the numinous beyond the self, and partly immanent within him," Also, "the spiritual side of man is not the product of intellectuality." In other words, the data from NDEs and other religious experiences indicate that the God of the panentheist is the Ultimate Reality; in *The God We Never Knew*, Marcus Borg makes a strong case for panentheism being biblical.

2. Judgment is a reality. In the NDE, the experiencer is often brought before a divine judge/being of light for a "life review." This can be frightening, comforting, or both; nevertheless, it is awesome. Judgment is virtually universal in world religions.

3. Hell is not permanent. Hell is for purification and rehabilitation and not eternal punishment. In *Universalism, the Prevailing Doctrine of the Christian Church During Its First 500 Years*, J. W. Hanson makes a good case that universalism was the dominant theology of early Christianity. In the West, it has been relegated to a minority position for the past 1500 years; nevertheless, it is the norm in the religions of the East (e.g., Hinduism, Buddhism).

   Whether they use the word "universalism" or not, a large number of NDE and/or religious experience researchers have come to the conclusion that ALL people are unconditionally loved by God and that, in the end, ALL will be "saved" regardless of religion or denomination. But there is also a dark side. Nancy Evans Bush offers her analysis of distressing NDEs using 21 studies (N=1,828) in *The Handbook of Near-Death Experiences: Thirty Years of Investigation* by J. Holden, B. Greyson, & D. James. Nine of these studies had no distressing NDEs, but the remaining 12 had a 23% rate of distressing NDEs. One of her blockbuster findings was that anyone (not just "evil" people) can face a "time of trial." Evidence that hell is not permanent includes the fact that NDErs are rescued from hell when they call out to God (or in the West, Jesus).

One very interesting case regarding the impermanence of hell is that of an eighteenth century near-death experiencer, Dr. George DeBenneville, who died of a consumptive-like illness and revived 42 hours later at his wake. During his tour of heaven and hell, he saw angels taking people out of hell and into heaven when they had repented. A full account of this experience is in Chapter 13. Both George Richey in his book *Return from Tomorrow* and Raymond Moody in his book *Reflections on Life After Life* report accounts of people trapped in negative/hellish states as having beings of light standing by them, waiting to rescue them. James McClenon in his book *Wondrous Events* describes a seventh century Japanese account of a butcher having a hellish deathbed vision which turns positive when he begins chanting the name of the Amida Buddha. Merete Jakobsen notes in *Negative Spiritual Encounters* that the antidote for negative spiritual experiences is prayer and religious rituals.

4. <u>JESUS is not an only child.</u> Jesus is called "the only begotten son" four times in the Gospel of John and one time in the first Letter of John, but none of the other New Testament writers mention this. There are also a number of Bible verses which indicate that God is the King of the gods (Ps 82:1, Dan 2:47, I Cor 8:5). While non-Christians sometimes encounter Jesus in their NDEs and mystical experiences, they also report encounters with other divine entities. Divine beings that individuals encounter are discussed in *Religious Experience in Contemporary China* by Xingong Yao and Paul Badham and in *At the Hour of Death* by Karlis Osis and Erlendur Harldsson. The latter book compares the deathbed visions and NDEs of people in India and the United States.

5. <u>What's in your heart, not what you believe, is what counts.</u>
    Religious groups that declare that theirs is the only path to
    God and salvation are totally wrong. NDE and other religious
    experiences (e.g., after-death communications, death-bed visions)
    are replete with stories of people of all faiths and denominations
    in heaven.

6. <u>"By their fruits you shall know them."</u> Virtually all of the books
    on the NDE and other religious experiences mentioned in this
    article speak to the fact that these events change people for the
    better, with some authors devoting a whole chapter to this finding.

7. <u>The NDE points to mind-body dualism.</u> In the *Handbook of
    Near-Death Experiences: Thirty Years of Investigation,* Jan Holden
    notes that attempts to place targets in hospitals for NDErs to see
    during their out-of-body experiences have been unsuccessful to
    date; however, the sheer volume of veridical perception anecdotes
    over 150 years demonstrates the reality of NDErs being out of
    their bodies. Additional evidence for mind-body dualism is
    presented in E.F. Kelly et.al.'s *Irreducible Mind* and Tim van
    Lommel's *Consciousness Beyond Life.*

8. <u>Reincarnation is the unanswered question.</u> Reincarnation is
    an essential part of the belief system of Eastern religions. The
    "official" position in Western religions is "no" (although a quarter
    of Christians in the UK and USA tell us that they believe this).
    The data supporting reincarnation is beginning to come in, as
    this is a major research area at the University of Virginia Medical
    School's Division of Perceptual Studies. Jim Tucker's book *Life
    Before Life* is based on 2,500 cases of reported reincarnation
    from the division's files.

9. <u>NDE is not without its skeptics.</u> The NDE has attracted numerous
    detractors, many of whom offer only explanations rather than
    data. An excellent refutation of questions raised by major skeptics
    of the NDE can be found in Bruce Greyson's chapter on the
    topic in the *Handbook of Near-Death Experiences: Thirty Years
    of Investigation.*

Conclusion

Research into the NDE and other spiritual experiences broadens our understanding of God and afterlife and serves as an essential counter to the oppressive religion that is all too common in today's world. Thanks to research over the past 150 years, we currently know more about how humans experience God and afterlife than at any time in recorded history. The picture emerging is of a generic God and afterlife that are universal; its essential elements are an "off-the-rack" fit for all the world's religions but a "tailor-made" fit for none of them. What is universal is from God; the remainder of religion is cultural. I pray that we continue this research.

APPENDIX

THE SALVATION CONSPIRACY:

How Hell Became Eternal

Universal Salvation is the theological position that ALL people will be saved. This concept, present from the earliest days of Christianity, is supported by numerous verses in the Bible, second in number only to those advocating Salvation by Good Works. Universalists do not reject the undeniable fact that Hell is in the Bible but contend that the function of Hell is for purification. Much later in the Christian story, when some claimed that Hell was a place for everlasting punishment, Universalists countered with their conviction that God was too good to condemn anyone to Eternal Hell! Today's world news is saturated with the tragedies resulting from religions that insist on their own "exclusive" path to God, and Universalists are reasserting the relevance of that loving doctrine known to the earliest Christians - Salvation for ALL.

In this paper, I will attempt to make the following points clear:

1. For the first 500 years of Christianity, Christians and Christian theologians were broadly Universalist.
2. Translation/Mistranslation of the Scriptures from Greek to Latin contributed the reinterpretation of the nature of Hell.

3. Merging of Church and State fostered the corruption of Universalist thought.
4. Modern archeological findings and Biblical scholarship confirm Universalist thought among early Christians.
5. Contemporary Christian scholars find Universalist theology most authentic to Jesus.

To examine Universal Salvation during the first 500 years of Christianity, the works of three scholars are indisputably the finest: Hosea Ballou II's *Ancient History of Universalism* (1842), Edward Beecher's *History of Opinions on the Scriptural Doctrine of Retribution* (1878), and John Wesley Hanson's *Universalism, the Prevailing Doctrine of the Church for its First 500 Years* (1899). I have used all these resources but have broadened Universalist history to include twentieth century discoveries and scholarship pertinent to Universalist Christianity.

In the Beginning

At its beginning, Christianity was a hopeful religion. In the words of St. Paul, "There is no longer Jew or Greek, there is no longer slave or free, there is no longer male or female; for all of you are one in Christ Jesus" (Gal 3:28). Communal meals, a culture of sharing and a tradition of helping others were the hallmarks of the early church. Despite a paternalistic culture, women were Apostles (Lk 8:2-3) and ministers (Rom 16: 1). One of the best clues to early Christian theology is in artwork discovered at the Catacombs in Rome. Graves of common people were adorned with drawings of Jesus as the Good Shepherd - beardless and virtually indistinguishable from the Greco-Roman savior figure Orpheus. Other popular images there were the Last Supper and the Magi at the birth of Jesus. Occasionally in early Christian art, Jesus is shown working miracles using a magic wand! Significantly, the crucifix is noticeably absent from early art, as is any depiction of judgment scenes or Hell.

As we move into the middle of the second century, a shift takes place from writing works considered "Holy Scripture" to interpretations of it. The first writer on the theology on Christian Universalism whose works survive is St. Clement of Alexandria (150 - 215CE). He was the head of the theology school at Alexandria which, until it closed at the end of the fourth century, was a bastion of Universalist thought. His pupil, Origen (185 - 254 CE), wrote the first complete presentation of Christianity as a system, and Universalism was at its core. Origen was the first to produce a parallel Old Testament that included Hebrew, a Greek transliteration of the Hebrew, the Septuagint, and three other Greek translations. He was also the first to recognize that some parts of the Bible should be taken literally and others metaphorically. He wrote a defense of Christianity in response to a pagan writer's denigration of it.

Prior to the Roman Catholic Church's condemnation of all of Universalist thought in the sixth century, Church authority had already reached back in time to pick out several of Origen's ideas they deemed unacceptable. Some that found disfavor were his insistence that the Devil would be saved at the end of time, the pre-existence of human souls, the reincarnation of the wicked, and his claim that the purification of souls could go on for many eons. Finally, he was condemned by the Church because his concept of the Father, Son, and Holy Spirit did not agree with the "official" Doctrine of the Trinity formulated a century after his death! After the sixth century, much of his work was destroyed; fortunately, some of it survived.

According to Edward Beecher, a Congregationalist theologian, there were six theology schools in Christendom during its early years - four were Universalist (Alexandria, Cesarea, Antioch, and Edessa). One advocated annihilation (Ephesus) and one advocated Eternal Hell (the Latin Church of North Africa). Most of the Universalists throughout Christendom followed the teachings of Origen. Later, Theodore of Mopsuestia had a different theological basis for Universal Salvation, and his view continued in the breakaway Church of the East (Nestorian) where his Universalist ideas still exist in its liturgy today.

"Harrowing of Hell" in Cannon and Apocrypha

One of the primary beliefs of the early Christians was that Jesus descended into Sheol/Hades in order to preach to the dead and rescue all of those, as it clearly says in I Peter 3:20, "who in former times did not obey." This terminology is familiar to anyone who has recited the Apostle's Creed which states that Jesus descended to Hell after his death, before his resurrection. Known as the "Harrowing of Hell," this is a major theme in Universalism because it underscores the early belief that judgment at the end of life is not final and that all souls can be saved after death. Interestingly, in the early Church there were not only prayers for the dead, but St. Paul notes there were also baptisms for the dead (I Cor 15: 29). In later times, the church attempted to reinterpret the text to narrow the categories of people saved from Hell to the Jewish prophets and the righteous pagans. Marcus Borg and John Dominic Crossan take this approach in their latest book, *The Last Week*. (Curiously, they omit the key verse "those who in former times did not obey.")

However, in his earlier book, *The Cross That Spoke*, John Dominic Crossan is more favorable to the Universalist view. For example, he relates a story from the non-canonical Gospel of Peter in which two angels come down from Heaven to get Jesus out of the tomb on Easter morning. As they are carrying him out and are about to ascend to Heaven, a voice from Heaven asks them, "Hast thou preached to them that sleep?" The wooden cross that is somehow following them out of the tomb speaks and says, "Yes!" In discussing Jesus' decent into Hell, Crossan also sites another classic Universalist text, I Peter 4:6 which says, "For this is why the Gospel was preached even to the dead, that though they were judged in flesh like men they might live in the spirit like God." He also notes that in Colossians 2:15, Jesus, "disarmed the principalities and powers and made a public example of them," and in Ephesians 4:8-9: Therefore it is said, "When he ascended on high, he made captivity itself a captive; he gave gifts to his people." (When it says, "He ascended," what does it mean but that he also descended into the lower parts of the earth? He who descended is the same one who ascended far above all heavens, so that he might fill all things.")

Understanding the role of the "Harrowing of Hell" has been expanded by recent archeological findings and modern Biblical scholarship. Among the discoveries over the past 100 years is the Apocalypse of Peter, written about 135 C.E. (not to be confused with the Gnostic Apocalypse of Peter discovered at Nag Hammadi in 1947). For a time, it was considered for inclusion into the New Testament instead of the Revelation to John. It is referred to in the Muratorian Canon of the early Church, as well as in the writings of St. Clement of Alexandria. (It should be noted that the Universalist passage from the Apocalypse of Peter is found in the Ethiopian text but is not part of the fragment text found at Akhmim, Egypt.) In the Ethiopic copy, Peter asks Jesus to have pity on the people in Hell, and Jesus says they will eventually all be saved. Later, Peter (who is writing to Clement) says to keep that knowledge a secret so that foolish men may not see it. This same theme is repeated in the *Second Book of the Sibyline Oracles* in which the saved behold the sinners in Hell and ask that mercy be shown them. Here, the sinners are saved by the prayers of the righteous.

Another second century work, The Epistle to the Apostles, also states that our prayers for the dead can affect their forgiveness by God. The second-century *Odes of Solomon*, which was discovered in the early twentieth century, was for a time considered to be Jewish, then Gnostic, and more recently, early Christian. Its theme is that Jesus saves the dead when they come to him in Hell and cry out, "Son of God, have pity on us!" In the fourth/sixth-century Syriac *Book of the Cave of Treasures*, Jesus "preached the resurrection to those who were lying in the dust" and "pardoned those who had sinned against the Law." In the Gospel of Nicodemus (a.k.a. Acts of Pilate), a fourth/fifth century apocryphal gospel, Jesus saves everyone in the Greek version but rescues only the righteous pre-Christians in the Latin translation. In *What is Gnosticism?*, Karen King identifies the Nag Hammadi Gospel of Truth as teaching Universal Salvation; she states that The Apocryphon of John (a.k.a. The Secret Book of John) declares all will be saved except apostates. In the Coptic Book of the Resurrection, all but Satan and his ministers are pardoned.

Interestingly, belief in the "Harrowing of Hell" has had some validation by modern day near-death experiencers (people who have been resuscitated following a period of clinical death). While most near-death experiencers report a "heavenly" experience of Light and overwhelming love, many of those whose experience begins in "hellish" turmoil and darkness say that their descent was reversed when they called out to God or Jesus.

The Church-State Conundrum

Many think that Christianity was at its best during its first 300 years - a time of immense diversity of opinion, creativity, and expectation. Although the official sanction of governments provided the Church with some very critical benefits (like not feeding Christians to lions!), some of the vitality of the young Church was inevitably compromised. Its legitimization in the fourth century, first by the king of Armenia, then by Constantine of Rome, and finally by the king of Ethiopia, led to a new era for Christianity. Constantine, being a military man, wanted standardization in all things. The Emperor called the Counsel of Nicea because at the time, the Bishop of Rome was not yet Pope (in the way we think of him today). According to Roman Catholic scholar Jean-Guy Vaillancourt, the Pope did not become the head of the Roman Church until 752 CE. At that time, Charlemagne recognized the Bishop of Rome as the singular Pope, and Pope Leo III reciprocated by legitimizing Charlemagne as the Holy Roman Emperor. It should be noted that the sixth-century Emperor Justinian - NOT the Bishop of Rome - called the Church counsel where Universalism was condemned.

Jesus Seminar "Endorses" Christian Universalism

Of all modern Biblical scholars, none have gained so much publicity and been so readily accessible to the lay reader than a group called the Jesus Seminar. Over 150 Biblical scholars pooled their knowledge for the express purpose of analyzing the Gospels to determine which words and deeds were authentic to Jesus. Their resulting "Scholars' Edition" of the Gospels were remarkable for the few passages that were thought to be original to Jesus. For Universalists, the most significant result of the Seminar's scrutiny was their inadvertent highlighting of many Universalist passages. By far, verses advocating Universal Salvation received the most endorsement from the Jesus Seminar as authentic to Jesus. While they rejected some of the "zingers" (e.g., Jn 12:32), virtually all Jesus' classic parables that have been interpreted as Universalist since the beginning of Christian theology were judged by the Jesus Seminar to be genuine to him, including: The Parable of the Lost Sheep (Matt 18:12-13; Lk 15:4-6), The Workers in the Vineyard (Matt 20:1-15), The Parable of the Lost Coin (Lk 15:8-9), and the Parable of the Prodigal Son (Lk 15:11-32). Also, the verses relating to the fact that Hell is not permanent and used only for rehabilitation/purification were determined authentic by the Jesus Seminar. They are: Settle with Your Opponent (Matt 5:25 -26; Lk 12:58 -59) and the Parable of the Wicked Servant (Matt 18:23 -34). Finally, although it was mutilated in part by the Jesus Seminar scholars, Jesus' teaching to be like God and love our enemies as God is good to the just and the unjust (Matt 5:44-46) was voted genuine to Jesus. It is noteworthy that the Seminar rejected all of the verses relating to the "Jesus Saves" theology as original to Jesus. John Calvin's Predestination fared only slightly better with only two verses seen as original to Jesus (Matt 6:10, 10:29). Some classic sayings of Jesus on Good Works were deemed authentic, such as Parable of the Good Samaritan (Luke 10:30 -35), Jesus on forgiveness (Matt 6:12), and the Parable of the Sower (Mk 4:3-8; Matt 13:3-8; Lk 8:5-8).

Mistranslations and Misanthropes

One of the essential tenents of Universalism is that all punishment in Hell is remedial, curative, and purifying. As long as Western Christianity was mainly Greek - the language of the New Testament - it was Universalist.

Interestingly, NONE of the Greek-speaking Universalists ever felt the need to explain Greek words such as "aion" and "aionion." In Greek, an aion (in English, usually spelled "eon") is an indefinite period of time, usually of long duration. When it was translated into Latin Vulgate, "aion" became "aeternam" which means "eternal." These translation errors were the basis for much of what was written about Eternal Hell.

The first person to write about Eternal Hell was the Latin North African Tertullian who is considered the Father of the Latin Church. As most people reason, Hell is a place for people you don't like to go! Tertullian fantasized that not only the wicked would be in Hell but also every philosopher and theologian who ever argued with him! He envisioned a time when he would look down from Heaven at those people in Hell and laugh with glee!

By far, the main person responsible for making Hell eternal in the Western Church was St. Augustine (354-430 CE). Augustine's Christian mother did not kick him out of her house for not marrying the girlfriend he got pregnant, but she did oust him when he became a Manichean Gnostic. Later, he renounced Manichaeism and returned to the Roman Church where he was made Bishop of Hippo in North Africa. He did not know Greek, had tried to study it, but stated that he hated it. Sadly, it is his misunderstanding of Greek that cemented the concept of Eternal Hell in the Western Church. Augustine not only said that Hell was eternal for the wicked but also for anyone who wasn't a Christian. So complete was his concept of God's exclusion of non-Christians that he considered un-baptized babies as damned; when these babies died, Augustine softened slightly to declare that they would be sent to the "upper level" of Hell. Augustine is also the inventor the concept of "Hell Lite", a.k.a. Purgatory, which he developed to accommodate some of the Universalist verses in the Bible. Augustine acknowledged the Universalists whom he called "tender-hearted," and included them among the "orthodox."

At this point, it should be noted that many in the early Church who were Universalist cautioned others to be careful whom they told about Universalism, as it might cause some of the weaker ones to sin. This has always been a criticism of Universalism by those who think that people will sin with abandon if there is no threat of eternal punishment. In fact, modern psychology has affirmed that love is a much more powerful motivator than fear, and knowing that God loves each and every person on the planet as much as God loves you does not promote delinquency.

Conversely, it is Christian exclusivity that leads to the marginalization of other human beings and the thinking that war and cruelty to the "other" are justified since they're going to Hell anyway! This kind of twisted thinking led to the persecution of the pagans, the witch hunts, the Inquisition, and the Holocaust.

Universalism in the East and Zoroastrian Roots

A slightly different type of Universalist theology was taught in the Aramaic speaking Church of the East (Nestorian). Virtually all of the Greek-speaking Universalists built on Origen's system that emphasizes free will. Origen saw an endless round of purification and relapse, but that in the end, God's love would draw all back to God. According to Dr. Beecher, Theodore of Mopsuestia (350-428 CE) saw, "sin as an unavoidable part of the development and education of man; that some carry it to a greater extent than others, but that God will finally overrule it for their final establishment in good." Theodore of Mopsuestia is known in the Nestorian Church as "The Interpreter."

The fifth century with its ongoing feuding councils saw major splits in the Christian Church. The Coptic Church of Egypt and Ethiopia split in 451CE; the Armenian Church left about the same time; the Church of the East (Nestorian) left in 486 CE. At the time of the split, the Nestorian Church was larger in numbers than the Roman Church. It included all of the Sasanian Persian Empire (which stretched from the Euphrates to India), along the Silk Road through modern Kazakhstan, Turkmenistan, Uzbekistan, through Tibet, Mongolia, and into China. Additionally, it had established Christian churches in the south of India by the end of the second century. While it suffered under Moslem invasion in the seventh century, it continued to grow in the Far East until being virtually annihilated by Tamerlane in the fourteenth century. Today, only a quarter-million remain. The Nestorian Church continued to be Universalist for most of its history, and a Universalist liturgy written by Theodore of Mopsuestia is still in use today. Also, the *Book of the Bee* written in the thirteenth century by Bishop Solomon of Basra includes the Universalist teachings of Isaac, Diodorus, and Theodore in Chapter 60. We know from Martin Palmer in the *Jesus Sutras* that the Nestorians who proselytized in China in the early days had only two Christian books: the Gospel of Matthew and an early Christian prayer book known as the *Didache* or The Teachings of the Twelve Apostles.

The appeal of Christianity in the Far East was that Jesus could save you and take you to Paradise, avoiding the risk of an undesired reincarnation. Christopher Buck notes in his article, "The Universality of the Church of the East: How Persian Was Persian Christianity?" that the success of Christian conversions in the East may have been the affinity of Christianity with Zoroastrianism. Unlike Manichaeism and other Gnostic Christianity, Zoroastrianism (like Judaism, Christianity, and Islam) maintains that the world was created good and was corrupted by evil. In Zoroastrianism, the basic tenents are: God-Satan, Good-Evil, Light-Darkness, Angels-Demons, Death-Judgment, Heaven-Hell, and at the end of time, the resurrection of the body and life everlasting. Zoroaster was a Universalist, as he says in his *Hymns to God,* "If you understand these laws of happiness and pain which God has ordained, O Mortals, there is a long period of punishment for the wicked and reward for the pious, but thereafter *Eternal Joy shall rein forever"* (Y 30:11 emphasis added*).* In Zoroastrianism, while God is wholly good, there is no doctrine of forgiveness; your good deeds must always outnumber your bad deeds in order to avoid purification in Hell. Christianity brought Jesus' message that God forgives sins for the asking! Also, one doesn't need a priest as an intercessor or a sacrifice to obtain God's grace. This affinity is best illustrated in a thirteenth century Christmas liturgy of the Nestorian Church which states that, "The Magi (Zoroastrian priests) came. They opened their treasures and offered him (Jesus) their offerings as they were commanded by their teacher Zoroaster who prophesized to them." What is implicit in the Gospel of Matthew is explicit in this Nestorian liturgy. Zoroaster had predicted the coming of future saviors "from the nations" (e.g., countries other than Persia). If you wanted to make converts in a Zoroastrian world, the story of the Magi at the birth of Jesus was your entree.

Universalism Officially Condemned in the West

Although the Roman Church had condemned some of Origen's other ideas, his Universalism was never questioned, nor were the writings of any other Universalist. There were even Universalists among the Gnostics; although Gnosticism had been condemned heartily by the Church, Universalism had never been listed among their errors. If Universal Salvation were heretical, how could the Church explain all those avowed Universalists who had already been made Saints (St. Clement of Alexandria, St. Macrina the Younger and her brother, St. Gregory of Nyssa, and others)? As mentioned earlier, it was the Emperor Justinian who initiated the deed.

Universalism had never been officially condemned prior to Justinian's convening the Council of Constantinople in 553CE, but this momentous decision was made against a background of turmoil in the Church and Western civilization. Latin-speaking Christians in the Church began to overshadow the Greek-speakers, and the Nestorian Church of the East had recently split from the Catholic West. (In all fairness, the Latin Church was doing well to have anyone who could read Latin - much less Greek.) Less than eighty years earlier, the Western Roman Empire had fallen to pagan barbarians. The Roman Church had long before become the handmaiden of the State. What could be better for control in an age of superstition and fear than to make Hell eternal and Salvation possible only through the Church? Less than a century later, all of Christianity (Latin, Greek, Armenian, Coptic, as well as the Nestorian Church of the East) would be either partially or totally overrun by Moslem conquerors.

Conclusion

Compare the hopeful, positive art of the early Church in the Catacombs with the scenes of Hell and damnation on the wall of almost every Medieval Catholic Cathedral. These scenes were made even more terrifying by the Latin mistranslation of Jesus' Parable of the Sheep and Goats (Matt 25:31-46). In the West, Augustine trumped Origen, and what was an "eon" in the original Greek became "eternal" in Latin.

While Universalism continued in the Church of the East, in the West from the sixth century forward, it was relegated to the realm of mystics until the Reformation when the idea of Universal Salvation was resurrected. Universalism continues today as a theological position among a fair number of Christians in a variety of denominations. It is ripe for revival.

References

• American Psychiatric Association. (1980). *Diagnostic and statistical manual of mental disorders* (third ed.). Washington, DC: Author.

• Antia, K. (2005). Zarathushti view of death and afterlife. *FEZANA Journal*, 3, 32-36, 55.

• Argyle, M. (2000). *Psychology and religion: An introduction.* New York, NY: Routledge.

• Armstrong, C. (1976). *Evelyn Underhill (1875-1941): An introduction to her life and writings.* William B. Eerdmans.

• Armstrong, K, (1992). *Muhammad: A biography of the prophet.* San Francisco: HarperSanFrancisco.

• Assmann, J. (2005). *Death and salvation in ancient Egypt* (Lorton, D., trans.). Ithaca, NY: Cornell University Press.

• Atwater, P. M. H. (1992). Is there a hell? Surprising observations about the near-death experience. *Journal of Near-Death Studies*, 10, 149-160. Reprinted with Permission.

• Austin, M. (1931). *Experiences facing death.* Bobbs Merrill Pub.

• Ballou, H. (1842). *Ancient history of Universalism: From the time of the apostles to the Fifth General Council.* Forgotten Books. (Original work published in 1878).

• Barrett, W. F. (1926). *Deathbed visions.* London, England: Methuen.

• Basford, T. (1990). *Near-death experiences: An annotated bibliography.* New York, NY: Garland.

• Baym, N. (Ed.) (1998). *Norton anthology of American literature, vol. 1.* New York: W. W. Norton.

• Beardsworth, T. (1977). *A sense of presence: Phenomenology of certain kinds of visionary and ecstatic experience.* Religious Experience Research Centre.

• Beauregard, M. & O'Leary, D. (2008). *The spiritual brain: A neuroscientist's case for the existence of the soul.* HarperOne.

• Becker, C. B. (1982). The failure of Saganomics: Why birth models cannot explain near-death phenomena. Anabiosis - The *Journal for Near-Death Studies*, 2, 102-109. Reprinted with Permission.

• Bede (1907). *Bede's ecclesiastical history of England* (Giles, J. A., trans.). London, England: George Bell and Sons. (Original work published eighth century).

• Beecher, E. (2007). *History of opinions on the scriptural doctrine of retribution.* Kessinger Publishing, LLC.

• Benneville, G. (1882). *The life and trance of Dr. George De Benneville, of Germantown, Pa: An account of what he saw and heard during a trance of forty-two hours.* N. Bertolet Grubb.

• Benson, H., & Stark, M. (1997). *Timeless healing: The power and biology of belief.* New York, NY: Fireside.

• Bentall, R. P. (2000). Hallucinatory experiences. In E. Cardeña, S. J. Lynn, & S. Kripper (Eds.), *Varieties of anomalous experience: Examining the scientific evidence* (pp. 85-120). Washington, DC: American Psychological Association.

• Bhattacharji, S. (1987). Yama. In Eliade, M. (ed.), *Encyclopedia of religion, vol. 15* (pp. 496-497). New York, NY: Macmillan.

• Blackmore, S. (1983). Birth and the OBE: An unhelpful analogy. *Journal of the American Society for Psychical Research*, 77, 227-238.

• Bonda, J. (1998). *The one purpose of God: An answer to the doctrine of eternal punishment.* Grand Rapids, MI: William B. Eerdmans. (Original work published 1993).

• Borg, M. (1997). *The God we never knew: Beyond dogmatic religion to a more authentic contemporary faith.* San Francisco, CA: HarperSanFrancisco.

• Borg, M. (2001). *Reading the* Bible *again for the first time: Taking the* Bible *seriously but not literally.* San Francisco, CA: HarperSanFrancisco.

• Borg, M. & Crossan. J.D. (2006). *The last week: What the gospels really teach about Jesus' final days in Jerusalem.* HarperOne.

• Boyce, M. (1984). *Textual sources for the study of Zoroastrianism.* Chicago: The University of Chicago Press.

• Buck, C. (1996). The universality of the Church of the East: How Persian Was Persian Christianity? *Journal of the Assyrian Academic Society.*

• Bucke, R. M. (1931). *Cosmic consciousness: A study in the evolution of the human mind.* New York, NY: E. F. Dutton. (Original work published 1931).

• Budge, E, A, W, (1967/1895). *The Egyptian book of the dead: The papyrus of Ani in the British Museum.* New York: Dover Publications.

• Burnham, S. (1992). *A book of angels: Reflections on angels past and present and true stories of how they touch our lives.* Ballantine Books.

• Bush, N. E. (2002). Afterward: Making meaning after a frightening near-death experience. *Journal of Near-Death Studies,* 21 (2), 99-133. Reprinted with Permission.

• Bush, N. E. (2006). Distressing western near-death experiences: Research summary. Paper presented at the IANDS Conference, M.D. Anderson Hospital, Houston, Texas (DVD available from: iands.org).

• Cardeña, E., Lynn, S. J., & Krippner, S. (Eds.). (2000). Introduction: Anomalous experiences in perspective. In E. Cardeña, S. J. Lynn, & S. Krippner (Eds.), *Varieties of anomalous experience: Examining the scientific evidence* (pp. 3-21). Washington, DC: American Psychological Association.

• Casebolt, J. & Niekro, T. (2001). Some UU's are more U than U: Theological self-descriptors chosen by Unitarian Universalists. *Review of Religious Research.*

• Clarke, I. (Ed.). (2001). *Psychosis and spirituality: Exploring the new frontier.* Philadelphia, PA: Whurr.

• Coxhead, N. (1986). *The relevance of bliss: A contemporary exploration of mystic experience.* St Martins Pr.

• Cressy, J. (1994). *The near-death experience: Mysticism or madness.* Hanover, MA: Christopher.

• Cressy, J. (1996). *Mysticism and the near-death experience.* In L. W. Bailey & J. Yates (Eds.), *The near-death experience: A reader* (pp.369-384). New York, NY: Routledge.

• Crossan, J. D. (1998). *The birth of Christianity: Discovering what happened in the years immediately after the execution of Jesus.* New York, NY: Harper San Francisco.

• Crossan, J.D. (2008). *The cross that spoke: The origins of the passion narrative.* Wipf & Stock Pub.

• Daniels, M. (2004). Transpersonal psychologies. In C. Partridge (Ed.), *New religions: A guide: New religious movements, sects, and alternative spiritualities.* New York, NY: Oxford University Press.

• De Benneville, G. (1804). *The remarkable account of the life and trance of Doctor George de Benneville.* Philadelphia, PA: Thomas T. Stiles. (Available as U.S. Government Microform).

• Dunn, J. D. G. (1997). *Jesus and the spirit: A study of the religious and charismatic experience of Jesus and the first Christians as reflected in the New Testament.* Grand Rapids, MI: William B. Eerdmans. (Original work published 1975).

• Ellens, J. H. (2008). *Understanding religious experiences.* London, UK: Praeger.

• Ellwood, G. F. (2000) Religious experience, religious worldviews, and near-death studies. *Journal of Near-Death Studies,* 19, 5-21. Reprinted with Permission.

• Ellwood, G. F. (2001). *The uttermost deep: The challenge of painful near-death experiences.* New York, NY: Lantern Books.

• Evans-Wentz, W. Y. (ed.) (1957). *The Tibetan book of the dead: Or the after-death experiences on the bardo plane, according to Lama Kazi Dawa-Samdup's English Rendering.* London, England: Oxford University Press. (Original work published eleventh century).

• Farhat-Holzman, L. (2003). *Strange birds from Zoroaster's nest: An overview of revealed religion.* Nonetheless Press.

• Fenwick, P., & Fenwick, E. (1995). *The truth in the light.* New York, NY: Berkley Books.

• Fenwick, P., & Fenwick, E. (2008). *The art of dying.* New York, NY: Continuum.

• Flotz, R. (2004) *Spirituality in the land of the noble: How Iran shaped the world's religions.* Oxford: Oneworld, p. 73.

• Fowler, J. (1981). *Stages of faith: The psychology of human development and the quest for meaning.* Harpercollins College Div.

• Fox, M. (2003). *Religion, spirituality and the near-death experience.* New York, NY: Routledge.

• Fox, M. (2008). *Spiritual encounters with unusual light phenomena: Lightforms.* Cardiff, Wales: University of Wales Press.

• Freeman, J. (2007). Levitate the Pentagon - retrieved from (Jan 7, 2007): www.jofreeman.com/photos/Pentagon67.html

• Funk, R., & the Jesus Seminar. (1998). *The acts of Jesus: The search for the authentic deeds of Jesus.* New York, NY: HarperSanFrancisco.

• Funk, R., Hoover, R. W., & the Jesus Seminar. (1993). *The five gospels - What did Jesus really say? The search for the authentic words of Jesus.* New York, NY: HarperOne.

• George, T. (1997, December 8). The gift of salvation. *Christianity Today,* pp. 35-37.

• Glock, C. Y, and Stark, R (1965). *Religion and society in tension.* Chicago, IL: Rand McNally.

• Greeley, A. (1974). *Ecstasy: A way of knowing.* Englewood Cliffs, NJ: Prentice Hall.

• Gregory the Great (1959). *Gregory the Great: Dialogues* (Fathers of the Church) (O. J. Zimmerman, Trans.). New York, NY. (Original work published sixth century AD).

• Greyson, B. (2000). Near-death experiences. In Cardeña, E. S., Lynn, S. J., and Krippner, S. (eds.), *Varieties of anomalous experience: Examining the scientific evidence* (Dissociation, Trauma, Memory, and Hypnosis) (pp. 315-352). Washington, DC: American Psychological Association.

• Greyson, B., and Bush, N. E. (1992). Distressing near-death experiences. *Psychiatry,* 55, 95-110.

• Greyson, B., Kelly, E. W., & Kelly, E. F. (2009). Explanatory models for near-death experience. In Holden, J., Greyson, B., & James, D. (Eds.). *The handbook of near-death experiences: thirty years of investigation.* Santa Barbara, CA: Praeger/ABC-CLIO.

• Guggenheim, B., & Guggenheim, J. (1996). *Hello from heaven: A new field of research-after-death communication confirms that life and love are eternal.* New York, NY: Bantam Books.

• Gulley, P. & Mulholland, J. (2005). *If God is love: Rediscovering grace in an ungracious world.* HarperOne; Reprint edition.

• Gulley, P. & Mulholland, J. (2004). *If grace is true: Why God will save every person.* HarperOne.

• Habermas, G. (2012). Resurrection appearances of Jesus as after-death communication: Response to Ken Vincent. *Journal of Near-Death Studies,* 30(3), 148–157. Reprinted with Permission.

• Hanson, J. W. (1899). *Universalism, the prevailing doctrine of the Christian Church during its first five hundred years.* Boston, MA: Universalist Publishing House.

• Haraldsson, E. (2007). "Sai Baba and the Indian miracle makers" - retrieved from (Jan 7, 2007): www.hi.is/~erlendur/english/svid.htm#6

• Haraldsson, E. (2012). *The departed among the living: An investigative study of afterlife encounters.* Guildford, UK: White Crow Books.

• Hardy, A. (1997). *The spiritual nature of man: A study of contemporary religious experience.* Oxford, England: The Religious Experience Research Centre. (Original work published 1979).

• Hargrove, T. (1995). *Long march to freedom: Tom Hargrove's own story of his kidnapping by Colombian narco-guerrillas.* New York, NY: Ballantine Books.

• Harpur, T. (1986). *For Christ's sake.* Toronto, Canada: McClelland and Stewart.

• Harpur, T. (1991). *Life after death.* Toronto, Canada: McClelland & Stewart.

• Harpur, T. (2011). *There is life after death.* Toronto, Canada: Thomas Allen.

• Hastings, A., Ferguson, E., Hutton, M., Goldman, A., Braud, W., Greene, E., Steinbach-Humphrey, S. (2002). Psychomanteum research: Experiences and effects on bereavement. *Omega*, 45, 211-228.

• Hastings, J., Grant, F. C., and Rowley, H. H. (eds.). (1953). *Dictionary of the* Bible. New York, NY: Scribner's.

• Hay, D. (1987). *Exploring inner space: Scientists and religious experience.* London, England: Mowbray.

• Hay, D. (2007). *Something there: The biology of the human spirit.* Templeton Press.

• Hick, J. (1993a). *Disputed questions in theology and the philosophy of religion.* New Haven, CT: Yale University Press.

• Hick, J. (1993b). *The metaphor of God incarnate: Christology in a pluralistic age.* Louisville, KY: Westminster/John Knox Press.

• Hick, J. (1999). *The fifth dimension: An exploration of the spiritual realm.* Oxford, England: One World.

• Hick, J. (2005). *John Hick: An autobiography.* Oxford, England: One World.

• Hick, J. (2006). *The new frontier of religion and science: Religious experience, neuroscience, and the transcendent.* New York, NY: Palgrave Macmillan.

• Hick, J. (2008). *Who or what Is God?: And other investigations.* London, UK: SCM Press.

• Hick, J., Pinnock, C. H., McGrath, A. E., Geivett, R D., and Phillips, W.G. (1995). *More Than one way?: Four views on salvation in a pluralistic world.* Grand Rapids, MI: Zondervan.

• Holden, J., Greyson, B., & James, D. (Eds.). (2009). *The handbook of near-death experiences: Thirty years of investigation.* Santa Barbara, CA: Praeger/ABC-CLIO.

• Holmes, H. (2006). Religious experience in contemporary China. *De Numine*, 40(2), 33-34. Reprinted with Permission.

• Hood, R. W. (2001). *Dimensions of mystical experiences: Empirical studies and psychological links.* New York, NY: Rodopi.

• Hood, R. W., Spilka, B., Hunsberger, B., & Gorsuch, C. R. (1996). *The psychology of religion: An empirical approach* (second ed.). New York, NY: Guilford Press.

• Hood, R., Hill, P., & Spilka, B. (2009). *The psychology of religion*, fourth Ed. London: The Gilford Press.

• Horgan, J. (2003). *Rational mysticism: Dispatches from the border between science and spirituality.* New York, NY: Houghton Mifflin.

• Howe, C. A. (1993). *The larger faith: A short history of American Universalism.* Boston, MA: Skinner House.

• Hyslop, J. H. (1908). *Psychical research and the resurrection.* London, England: T. Fisher Unwin.

• International Association for Near-Death Studies. (2009). History and founders. Retrieved from www.iands.org/about_iands/iands/history.html

• Jakobsen, M. D. (1999). *Negative spiritual experiences: Encounters with evil.* Lampeter, Wales: Religious Experience Research Centre.

• James, W. (1994). *The varieties of religious experience.* New York, NY: Modern Library. (Original work published 1901).

• Jefferson, W. (2008). *Reincarnation beliefs of North American Indians, soul journeys, metamorphoses, and near-death experience.* Summertown, TN: Native Voices.

• Johnson, L. T. (1998). *Living Jesus: Learning the heart of the gospel.* New York, NY: HarperCollins.

• Johnson, L. T. (1998). *Religious experience in earliest Christianity: A missing dimension In* New Testament *studies*. Minneapolis, MN: Fortress Press.

• Jung, C. G. (1961). *Memories, dreams, reflections.* New York, NY: Pantheon Press.

• Kalish, R. A. & Reynolds, D. K. (1973). Phenomenological reality and post-death contact. *Journal for the Scientific Study of Religion*, 12,2, 209–221. Reprinted with Permission.

• Keller, J. C. (2005). Swedish scientists can't replicate religious experience in lab. Retrieved from www.varioustopics.com/alternative-medicine/1004033-swedish-scientists-cant-replicate-religious-experience-in-lab.html

• Kelly, E. W. & Kelly, E. F., et al. (2007). Toward a psychology for the twenty-first century. In E. F. Kelly, E. W. Kelly, A. Crabtree, A. Gauld, M. Grosso, & B. Greyson, *Irreducible mind: Toward a psychology for the twenty-first century* (pp. 577-643). New York, NY: Rowman & Littlefield.

• Kelly, E. W., Greyson, B., & Kelly, E. F. (2007). Unusual experiences near-death and related phenomena. In E. F. Kelly, E. W. Kelly, A. Crabtree, A. Gauld, M. Grosso, & B. Greyson, *Irreducible mind: Toward a psychology for the twenty-first century* (pp. 577-643). New York, NY: Rowman & Littlefield.

• King, K. (2005). *What is Gnosticism?* Belknap Press of Harvard University Press.

• Kircher, P. M. (1995). *Love is the link: A hospice doctor shares her experience of near death and dying.* Burdett, NY: Larson Publications.

• Kohlberg, L. (1981). *The philosophy of moral development: Moral stages and the idea of justice.* Harper & Row.

• Kroll, J., & Bachrach, B. (1982). Visions and psychopathology in the Middle Ages. *Journal of Nervous and Mental Disease*, 170, 41-49.

• Lead, J. (2010) *The Enochian walks with God, found out by a spiritual traveller.* Gale ECCO, Print Editions.

• Leary, T. (1983). *Flashbacks: An autobiography.* Los Angeles, CA: Jeremy P. Tarcher.

• Linn, D. & Linn, S. & Linn, M. (1993). *Good goats: Healing our image of God.* Paulist Press.

• Lommel, P. (2011). *Consciousness beyond life: The science of the near-death experience.* New York, NY: HarperOne.

• Long, J., & Perry, P. (2010). *Evidence of the afterlife: The science of near-death experiences.* New York, NY: HarperOne.

• Lundahl, C. R. (1981). *The perceived other world in Mormon near-death experiences: A social and physical description.* Omega, 12, 319-327.

• Masumian, F. (1995). *Life after death: A study of the afterlife in world religions.* Oxford, England: One World.

• Marsh, C. Receiving the call. Retrieved from: www.beliefnet.com/ Faiths/Christianity/2005/01/Receiving-The-Call.aspx

• Maslow, A. (1964). *Religions, values, and peak-experiences.* New York, NY: Viking Press.

• Maxwell, M., & Tschudin, V. (2005). *Seeing the invisible: Modern religious and other transcendent experiences.* Ceredigion, Wales: Religious Experience Research Centre. (Original work published 1990).

• McClenon, J. (1991). Near-death folklore in medieval China and Japan: A comparative analysis. *Asian Folklore Society, 50,* 319-342.

• McClenon, J. (1994). *Wondrous events: Foundations of religious beliefs.* Philadelphia, PA: University of Pennsylvania Press.

• McClenon, J. (2002). *Wondrous healing: Shamanism, human evolution, and the origin of religion.* DeKalb, IL: Northern Illinois University Press.

• Mehr, F. (2003). *The Zoroastrian tradition: An introduction to the ancient wisdom of Zarathushtra.* Mazda Pub.

• Merh, K. P. (1996). *Yama, the glorious lord of the other world.* New Delhi, India: D.K. Printworld.

• Meyer, M. W. (Ed.). (1987). *The ancient mysteries: A sourcebook of sacred texts.* San Francisco, CA: Harper & Row.

• Migliore, V. (2009). *A measure of heaven: Near-death experience data analysis.* Folsom, CA: Blossom Hill Books.

• Miller, R. J. (1995). *The complete gospels: Annotated scholar's version.* Polebridge Press.

• Mitofsky International and Edison Media Research. (2002). Exploring religious America. *Religion & Ethics Newsweekly,* May 10, 2002, Retrieved May 16, 2002, from: www.pbs.org/wnet/religionandethics/week534/ cover.html

• Modi, J. J. (2010). *A catechism of the Zoroastrian religion.* Nabu Press.

• Mojsov, B. (2005). *Osiris: Death and afterlife of a god.* Malden, MA: Blackwell.

• Moody, R. & Perry, P. (2010). *Glimpses of eternity: Sharing a loved one's passage from this life to the next.* Guideposts; Book Club Edition.

• Moody, R. (1975). *Life after life: The investigation of a phenomenon - survival of bodily death.* Covington, GA: Mockingbird Books.

• Moody, R. (1977). *Reflections on life after life.* Bantam.

• Moody, R. & Perry, P. (2012). *Paranormal: My life in pursuit of the afterlife.* New York, NY: HarperOne.

• Moody, R., & Perry, P. (1994). *Reunions: Visionary encounters with departed loved ones.* New York, NY: Ivy Books.

• Morgan, J. C. (1995). *The devotional heart: Pietism and the renewal of American Unitarian Universalism.* Boston, MA: Skinner House Books.

• Moulton, J. H. (1913). *Early Zoroastrianism.* London, England: Williams and Norgate, 1913.

• Müller, F. M. (Ed.). (1897). *Sacred books of the east.* Oxford, England: Oxford University Press.

• Murphy, T. (2006). Inner worlds, outer worlds. Retrieved from: www.innerworldsmovie.com

• Myers, F. W. H. (1915). *Human personality and its survival of bodily death* (Studies in consciousness). London, England: Logmans, Green. (Original work published 1903).

• Newberg, A., D'Aquili, E., & Rause V. (2001). *Why God won't go away: Brain science and the biology of belief.* New York, NY: Ballantine Books.

• Newsweek. (2009). God's miraculous makeover. *Newsweek,* 153(5), 12.

• Nigosian, S. A. (2000). *World religions: A historical approach* (third ed.). New York, NY: Bedford/St. Martin's.

• Oakes, K., & Gahlin, L. (2003). *Ancient Egypt: An illustrated reference to the myths, religion, pyramids, and temples of the land of the pharaohs.* New York, NY: Barnes & Noble.

• Origen. (1994). Origen de principiis. In Roberts, A. R., and Donaldson, J. (eds.) *Ante-Nicene Fathers, vol. 4* (pp. 260-279). Peabody, MA: Hendrickson Publishers. (Roberts and Donaldson original work published 1885).

• Osis, K., & Haraldsson, E. (1977). *At the hour of death: A new look at evidence for life after death.* New York, NY: Avon Books.

• Otto, R. (1950). *The idea of the holy: An inquiry into the non-rational factor in the idea of the divine and its relation to the rational.* New York, NY: Oxford University Press. (Original work published 1917).

• Oxman, T. E., Rosenberg, S. D., Schnurr, P. P., Tucker, G. J., & Gala, G. (1988). The language of altered states. *Journal of Nervous and Mental Disease*, 176, 401-408.

• Palmer, M. (2001). *The Jesus sutras: Rediscovering the lost scrolls of Taoist Christianity.* Wellspring/Ballantine.

• Partridge, C. (Ed.). (2004). *New religions: A guide: New religious movements, sects, and alternative spiritualities.* New York. NY: Oxford University Press.

• Pasricha, S. & Stevenson, I. (1986). Near-death experiences in India: A preliminary report. *Journal of Nervous and Mental Disease*, 174, 165-170.

• Perry, M. (2003). *Psychical and spiritual.* Lincolnshire: The Churches' Fellowship for Psychical and Spiritual Studies.

• Perry, M. C. (1959). *The Easter enigma: An essay on the resurrection with specific reference to the data of psychical research.* London, England: Faber & Faber.

• Phipps, W. E. (2008). *Supernaturalism in Christianity: Its growth and cure.* Macon, GA: Mercer University Press.

• Plato. (1892). *The dialogues of Plato* (Jowett, B., trans.). London, England: Humphrey Milford. (Original work published fourth century B.C.).

• Plutarch (1918). *Selected essays of Plutarch, vol. 2.* (Prickard, A. O., trans.). Oxford, England: Clarendon Press. (Original work published first century).

• Price, R. M. (2008). Brand x Easters. In B. B. Scott (Ed.), *The resurrection of Jesus: A sourcebook* (pp. 49–60). Santa Rosa, CA: Polebridge Press.

• Rankin, M. (2008). *An introduction to religious and spiritual experience.* London, England: Continuum International.

• Rawlings, M. S. (1978). *Beyond death's door.* Nashville, TN: Thomas Nelson.

• Riley, G. J. (2001). *The river of God: A new history of Christian origins.* New York, NY: HarperSanFrancisco.

• Ring, K. (1980). *Life at death: A scientific investigation of the near-death experience.* New York, NY: Coward, McCann, & Geoghegan.

• Ring, K. (1985). *Heading toward omega: In search of the meaning of the near-death experience.* Harper Perennial.

• Ring, K. (1986). From alpha to omega: Ancient mysteries and the near-death experience. Anabiosis - *Journal of Near-Death Studies*, 5, 3-15. Reprinted with Permission.

• Ring, K. (2000). Religious wars in the near-death movement: Some personal reflections on Michael Sabom's Light and Death. *Journal of Near-Death Studies*, 18, 214-244. Reprinted with Permission.

• Ring, K. (2005). Letter to the editor: Scope of IANDS and the journal. *Journal of Near-Death Studies*, 24, 51-52. Reprinted with Permission.

• Ring, K., & Valarino, E. E. (1998). *Lessons from the light: What we can learn from the near-death experience*. New York, NY: Insight Books.

• Ritchie, G. G., and Sherrill, E. (1978). *Return from tomorrow*. Old Tappan, NJ: Sprite.

• Ritchie, G.G. & Stevenson, I. (1998). *Ordered to return: My life after dying*. Charlottesville, VA: Hampton Roads Publishing Co.

• Robb, P. (2006). *The kindness of God: How God cares for us*. Outskirts Press.

• Roll, W. G. (2004). Psychomanteum research: A pilot study. *Journal of Near-Death Studies*, 22, 251-260. Reprinted with Permission.

• Rommer, B. R. (2000). *Blessing in disguise: Another side of the near-death experience*. St. Paul, MN: Llewellyn.

• Sabom, M. (1982). *Recollections of death: A medical investigation*. New York, NY: Harper & Row.

• Sabom, M. (1998). *Light and death: One doctor's fascinating account of near-death experiences*. Grand Rapids, MI: Zondervan.

• Sabom, M. (2000a). Response to Kenneth Ring's "Religious wars in the near-death movement: Some personal reflections on Michael Sabom's *Light and Death*." *Journal of Near-Death Studies*, 18, 245-271. Reprinted with Permission.

• Sabom, M. (2000b). Response to Gracia Fay Ellwood's "Religious experience, religious worldviews, and near-death studies." *Journal of Near-Death Studies*, 19, 23-44. Reprinted with Permission.

• Scott, B. B. (Ed.). (2008). *The resurrection of Jesus: A sourcebook*. Santa Rosa, CA: Polebridge Press.

• Segal, A. F. (2004). *Life after death: A history of the afterlife in the religions of the West*. New York, NY: Doubleday.

• Shushan, G. (2009). *Conceptions of afterlife in early civilizations: Universalism, constructivism, and near-death experience*. London, England: Continuum International.

• Siglag, M. A. (1986). Schizophrenic and mystical experiences: Similarities and differences (Doctorial dissertation). Retrieved from ProQuest. (AAT 8706811).

• Smith, H. (2000). *Cleansing the doors of perception: The religious significance of entheogenic plants and chemical.* New York, NY: Jeremy P. Tarcher/Putnam.

• Smith, H. (2011). *The unselfishness of God and how I discovered it.* Tentmaker Ministries & Publications, Inc.

• Sparrow, G. S. (1995). *I am with you always: True stories of encounters with Jesus.* New York, NY: Bantam Books.

• Sparrow, G. S. (2002). *Sacred encounters with Mary.* Notre Dame, IN: Ave Maria Press.

• Spence, L. (1990). *Ancient Egyptian myths and legends.* New York, NY: Dover. (Original work published 1915).

• Tabor, J.D. (2006). *The Jesus dynasty: The hidden history of Jesus, his royal family, and the birth of Christianity.* New York, NY: Simon & Schuster.

• Talbott, T. (1997). *The inescapable love of God.* Parkland, FL: Universal Publishers.

• Tamminen, K. (1991). *Religious development in childhood and youth: An empirical study.* Suomalainen Tiedeakatemia.

• Teiser, S. (1988). Having once died and returned to life: Representations of hell in medieval China. *Harvard Journal of Asiatic Studies*, p. 187.

• Tolle, E. (2004). *The power of now: A guide to spiritual enlightenment.* New World Library.

• Tucker, J. (2005). *Life before life: Children's memories of previous lives.* New York, NY: St. Martin's.

• Underhill, E. (2006). *Practical mysticism: A little book for normal people.* Cosimo Classics.

• Vaillancourt, J. (1980). *Papal power: A study of Vatican control over lay Catholic Elites.* Univ of California Pr.

• Vincent, K. R. & Morgan, J. (2006). An eighteenth century near-death experience: The case of George de Benneville. *Journal of near-death studies*, 25 (1), 35-48. Reprinted with Permission.

• Vincent, K. R. (1987). *The full battery codebook: A handbook for psychological test interpretation for clinical, counseling, rehabilitation, and school psychology.* Norwood, NJ: Ablex.

• Vincent, K. R. (1994). *Visions of God from the near-death experience.* Burdett, New York: Larson Publications.

• Vincent, K. R. (1999). *The Magi: from Zoroaster to the "three wise men."* North Richland Hills, Texas: Bibal Press.

• Vincent, K. R. (2000). Unitarian and Universalist concepts of salvation in the Bible and world religion. *Universalist Herald*, 152(5), 4-8.

• Vincent, K. R. (2003). The near-death experience and Christian Universalism. *Journal of Near-Death Studies*, 22, 57-71. Reprinted with Permission.

• Vincent, K. R. (2005). Magic, deeds, and Universalism: Afterlife in the world's religions. *Universalist Herald*, 156 (4), 5-8,12).

• Vincent, K. R. (2005). *The golden thread: God's promise of universal salvation.* New York, NY: iUniverse.

• Vincent, K. R. (2006). The salvation conspiracy: How hell became eternal. *Universalist Herald*. Retrieved from: www.christianuniversalist.org

• Vincent, K. R. (2007). Separating the "super" from the "natural." *De Numine*, 42, 5–8. Reprinted with Permission.

• Vincent, K. R. (2010a). Religious experience, Jesus, and modern research: An appraisal of the Jesus Seminar findings. *De Numine*, 49,10–12. Reprinted with Permission.

• Vincent, K. R. (2010b). The search for God and afterlife in the age of science. *Journal of Near-Death Studies*, 28(3), 123–141. Reprinted with Permission.

• Vincent, K. R. (2011). What the near-death experience and other spiritually transformative experiences teach us about God and afterlife. *De Numine*, 51, 9-13. Reprinted with Permission.

• Vincent, K. R. (2012). Resurrection appearances of Jesus as after-death communication. *Journal of Near-Death Studies*, 31, 30(3), 136–147. Reprinted with Permission.

• Walker, B. A., & Serdahley, W. J. (1990). Historical perspectives on near-death phenomena. *Journal of Near-Death Studies*, 9, 105-121. Reprinted with Permission.

• Weatherhead, L. (1990). *The Christian agnostic.* Abingdon Pr.

• Webb, M. (1985). Religious experience as doubt resolution. *International Journal for Philosophy of Religion.*

• West, D. J. (1995). Note on a recent psychic survey. *Journal of the Society for Psychical Research*, 60, 168-171.

• White, L. M. (2004). *From Jesus to Christianity: How four generations of visionaries and storytellers created the* New Testament *and Christian faith*. New York, NY: HarperSanFrancisco.

• Wiebe, P. H. (1997). *Visions of Jesus: Direct encounters from the* New Testament *to today*. New York, NY: Oxford University Press.

• Wiebe, P. H. (2000). Critical reflections on Christic visions. *Journal of Consciousness Studies, 7*, 119-141.

• Williams, K. R. (2002). *Nothing better than death: Insights from sixty-two profound near-death experiences*. Philadelphia, PA: Xlibris.

• Wolf, W. (1963). *The religion of Abraham Lincoln*. Seabury Press; Revised edition.

• Wood, F. W. (1989). *An American profile: Opinions and behavior 1972-1989*. Chicago, IL: National Opinion Research Center.

• Wood, S. E., & Wood, E. G. (1996). *The world of psychology* (second ed.). Boston, MA: Allyn & Bacon.

• Woodward, K. L. (2000). *The book of miracles: The meaning of miracle stories in Christianity, Judaism, Buddhism, Hinduism, and Islam*. London: Simon & Schuster.

• Wulff, D. M. (1997). *Psychology of religion* (second ed.). New York, NY: John Wiley & Sons.

• Yao, X & Badham, P. (2007). *Religious experience in contemporary China*. Cardiff: University of Wales.

• Yogi L.S. (2007). Rao attempts "walking on water." - retrieved from (Jan 7, 2007): www.killingthebuddha.com/mag/dogma/yoga-for-skeptics/

• Zaleski, C. (1987). *Otherworld journeys: Accounts of near-death experience in medieval and modern times*. New York, NY: Oxford University Press.

Permissions

All the chapters in *God Is With Us: What Near-Death and Other Spiritually Transformative Experiences Teach Us About God and Afterlife* were initially published in the form of articles printed elsewhere. The articles previously published in the *Journal of Near-Death Studies* and *De Numine* are reproduced with permission. For the remainder of the articles, The *Universalist Herald* was granted First North American Serial Rights.

Chapter 1: The Search for God and the Afterlife in the Age of Science

Originally published in *Journal of Near-Death Studies*, 28 (3), Spring 2010, reprinted with permission.

Chapter 2: Developmental Revelation

Originally published in *Universalist Herald*, 153, 5, September / October 2002.

Chapter 3: Ken's Guide to "Universals" In Religion

Originally published in *Universalist Herald*, 159, 5, September / October 2008.

Chapter 4: Separating the "Super" from the "Natural"

Originally published in *De Numine*, 42, Spring 2007, reprinted with permission.

Chapter 5: Religious Experiences of Jesus are Compatible with Modern Research

Originally published as "Religious Experience, Jesus, and Modern Research: An appraisal of the Jesus Seminar Findings" in *De Numine*, 49, Autumn 2010, reprinted with permission.

Chapter 6: Resurrection Appearances of Jesus as After-Death Communication

Originally published in *Journal of Near-Death Studies*, 30 (3), Spring 2012, reprinted with permission.

Chapter 7: Resurrection Appearances of Jesus as After-Death Communication (Rejoiner)

Originally published in *Journal of Near-Death Studies*, 30 (3), Spring 2012, reprinted with permission.

Chapter 8: Religious Experience Research Reveals Universalist Principles

Originally published as Religious "Experience and Universalism" in *Universalist Herald*, 160, 1, Winter 2010.

Chapter 9: Mystical Religious Experiences and Christian Universalism

Originally published as Chapter 7, *The Golden Thread, God's Promise of Universal Salvation* by Ken R. Vincent, 2005.

Chapter 10: The Near-Death Experience and Christian Universalism

Originally published in *Journal of Near-Death Studies*, 22(1), Fall 2003, reprinted with permission.

Chapter 11: An eighteenth century Near-Death Experience: The Case of George de Benneville

Originally published in *Journal of Near-Death Studies*, 25 (1), Fall 2006, reprinted with permission.

Chapter 12: Zoroaster: The Prophet of the Magi and the First Universalist

Originally published in *Universalist Herald*, 158, 3, May / June 2007.

Chapter 13: Omar Khayyam: Sufi Universalist

Originally published in *Universalist Herald*, 158, 5, September / October 2007.

Chapter 14: Universal Salvation in Hinduism and Its Children

Originally published as "Hindu and Buddhist Universalism" in *Universalist Herald*, 160, 3, Summer 2010.

Chapter 15: A Scientific Investigation of the "Dark Side"

Originally published as "Dark Side STEs" in *Universalist Herald*, 160, 3, May / June 2009.

Chapter 16: Magic, Deeds, and Universalism: The Afterlife in World Religions

Originally published in *Universalist Herald*, 156, 4, July / August 2005.

Chapter 17: What NDEs and Other Spiritually Transformative Experiences Teach Us About God and the Afterlife

Originally published in *DeNumine*, No. 51 (9-13), autumn 2011.

Appendix: The Salvation Conspiracy How Hell Was Made Eternal

Originally published in the July/August 2006 issue of *The Universalist Herald*

Unless otherwise noted all Bible quotations are from the *New Revised Standard Version* (NRSV), Copyright 1989, National Council of Churches of Christ, reproduced by permission

About the Author

~

D r. Ken R. Vincent has a B.Sc. in Psychology and a M.Ed. in Counseling from the University of Houston and an Ed.D. in Counseling Psychology from the University of Northern Colorado. Ken has had three careers in psychology — first as a counselor (in the War on Poverty programs of the Kennedy/Johnson administrations), second as a psychologist (working at Texas Rehabilitation Commission and the Hauser Psychiatry and Neurology Clinic), and third as a professor (Educational Psychology Dept. at the University of Houston and Houston Community College). In 1993, he married the love of his life Pam who became his best friend and first editor.

Concurrent with his career in psychology and continuing after his retirement in 2001, Ken had an avocational career as a writer and religious/spiritual experience researcher and lay Universalist minister. He has been active in interfaith organizations and the Foundation for Contemporary Theology; he served many years as webmaster for the *Universalist Herald*. He is the author of Visions *of God from the Near-Death Experience* (1994), *The Magi: From Zoroaster to the "Three Wise Men"* (1999), *The Golden Thread: God's Promise of Universal Salvation* (2005), *and God Is With Us: What Near-Death and Other Spiritually Transformative Experiences Teach Us About God and Afterlife* (2014 Online Version and 2019, White Crow Books).

Printed in June 2019
by Rotomail Italia S.p.A., Vignate (MI) - Italy